A Pictorial History of Williams Bay, Wisconsin

On Beautiful Geneva Lake

1836-1939

MICHELLE BIE LOVE
DEBORAH DUMELLE KRISTMANN
WILLIAMS BAY HISTORICAL SOCIETY

Copyright 2017
Williams Bay Historical Society

ISBN-13: 978-1548461201
ISBN-10: 1548461202

Edition 1.1 8/17

Published by Williams Bay Historical Society

THE WILLIAMS BAY HISTORICAL SOCIETY

The purpose of the Williams Bay Historical Society is to assist in the preservation and exhibition of items of historical interest that are within the boundaries of Williams Bay and the immediate surrounding area. The Society will seek to provide the public with educational opportunities to learn about our unique local history. The Society will also seek to organize and assist in the commemoration of significant dates and events in village history.

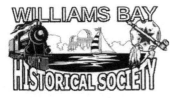

For all general information, please contact Williams Bay Historical Society.
P.O. Box 678
Williams Bay, WI 53191
Email wmsbayhistoricalsociety@gmail.com
Visit us on the Internet at http://wmsbayhistory.org

Disclaimer: Although the authors and publisher have made every effort to ensure that the information in this book is accurate and correct at press time, the authors and publisher do not assume and hereby disclaim any liability to any part for any loss, damage, or disruption caused by errors or omissions, whether such errors or omissions result from negligence, accident, or any other cause.

On the Cover: Frank Jr. (left) and Laddie Fleishman with an unidentified girl having fun at the bathhouse in Williams Bay. This photograph is from Filimena Fleishman Killar's album Williams Bay Family Summers at the Cottage from 1927-1952. Photo credit: Phyllis Killar Janda.

DEDICATION

A Pictorial History of Williams Bay, Wisconsin on Beautiful Geneva Lake is dedicated to the men, women, and children who helped to form Williams Bay from the first settlers in the 1830s to the present. The residents of the Village of Williams Bay have long exhibited a strong sense of community spirit.

We are proud to call Williams Bay home.

Acknowledgments

Gathering the material for *A Pictorial History of Williams Bay, Wisconsin on Beautiful Geneva Lake* has been a true labor of love for Michelle and Deborah. They would like to thank those individuals and organizations who enthusiastically shared their time, knowledge, photos, and/or collections. Compiling a historical account as such would be impossible without their contributions. Michelle and Deb are also grateful to family, friends and neighbors who have supported their efforts on this journey.

A Pictorial History of Williams Bay, Wisconsin on Beautiful Geneva Lake seeks to be the first work to give an accurate account of the people and the historical events in Williams Bay. The combination of the written facts and memories coupled with photographs presents a picture which otherwise would be incomplete.

We have made every effort to make this book accurate and are indebted to the individuals and organizations that have assisted in this endeavor:

Albert Allison, Bill Anderson, John A. Anderson, Nancy Snidtker Baldwin, Rick Barribeau, Kathy Batten, Judy Bausch, Paul L. Behrens, Rick Blakeley, George Blakslee, Lisa Hanson Brellenthin, Curt Carlson, Sheila Cisko, Delap Family, Kate Morris Dickerson Family, John and Joan Dumelle, Robert Franzen, Don and Lois Frederickson, George and Mary Goodlow, Louis Grell Family, Pat Grove, Carl Hanley, Tim Hanson, Dwight Heat Photography, Guri Henderson, Kristin Rees Hunsaker, Phyllis Killar Janda, Lynn "Gabby" Jensen, Catsy and Julie Johnson, Ruth Karkow, Kurt Kristmann, Mary C. Kristmann, Calvin Kuder, Tom and Kathy Leith, Richard Lidinsky, David Love, Magen Love, Annette Mann, Joan Elsner Miller, Jim Moeller, Edie O'Brien, Mary O'Brien and Joe Makowski, Carol Stenstrom Ortiz, Keith and Penny Pozulp, Penne Rush, Carolyn Smeltzer, Deb Soplanda, George Sorensen, John and Glendia Strandin, Terry Thomas, Warren Thornley, David Valley, and James Wallace Collection.

Ashfield (Massachusetts) Historical Society [Nancy Gray Garvin], Barrett Memorial Library [Ann Becker and Joy Schnupp], Bay Leaves, Big Foot Country Club [Melva Breitenstein], Board of Commissioners of Public Lands, Chicago Historical Society, Chicago Daily Tribune, Chicago Tribune, Conference Point, Congress Club [Carol Carlson Swed], Crystal Lake Historical Society, Forest County Potawatomi Cultural Center, Gage Marine [Maggie and Rachel Gage], Geneva Lake Museum, History of the Indian Tribes of North America, Holiday Home [Bradley Cripe], Lake Geneva Library, Lake Geneva Yacht [John and Kathy DeCarlo], Maps of Antiquity, Michigan State University, Milwaukee Journal, Norman B. Barr Camp [Tom Sergenian], United Church of Christ (Congregational)-Williams Bay, Walworth County Historical Society, Williams Bay Historical Society, Williams Bay Observer, Williams Bay School District and Alumni Association, Wisconsin Milk Marketing Board, Wisconsin State Historical Society, Wisconsin Veterans Museum, University of Chicago Library Archives, and Yerkes Observatory.

TABLE OF CONTENTS

U.S. and Geneva Lake Timeline...II

MAPS..IV

ODE TO WILLIAMS BAY...IX
GURI HENDERSON 2010

INTRODUCTION 1
HISTORY OF THE AREA 1836-1939

CHAPTER 1: THE HEART OF THE VILLAGE.........................35
LOCAL BUSINESSES/PROPRIETORS/FIRE DEPARTMENT

BREEZES FROM GENEVA LAKE......................................58
GEORGE C. BLAKSLEE 1892

CHAPTER 2: LAKE FRONT ACCESS..................................59
SHORE PATH/TRANSPORTATION/INDUSTRY

CHAPTER 3: HERITAGE OF YEAR-ROUND RECREATION...............91
BOATING/SWIMMING/FISHING/SAILING

CHAPTER 4: YERKES OBSERVATORY................................121
EYES AROUND THE WORLD TURN TO WILLIAMS BAY

CHAPTER 5: HOME SWEET HOME 139
SETTLERS/INFLUENTIAL PEOPLE/ASSOCIATIONS

CHAPTER 6: A PICTURE OF LIFE IN THE BAY......................175
IMAGES BY PHOTOGRAPHER GEORGE BLAKSLEE AND OTHERS

CHAPTER 7: PILLARS OF THE COMMUNITY.........................193
CHURCHES/SCHOOLS/ORGANIZATIONS

CHAPTER 8: VACATION GETAWAY...................................209
RESORTS/HOTELS/BOARDING HOUSES

CHAPTER 9: FRESH AIR RETREATS.................................221
CAMPS/RELIGIOUS CONFERENCES

CHAPTER 10: GENEVA LAKE HISTORICAL SOCIETY..................239
CENTENNIAL CELEBRATION 1831-1931

BIBLIOGRAPHY...252

ABOUT THE AUTHORS...254

U.S. AND GENEVA LAKE TIMELINE

1829-1837 Andrew Jackson
1830 Indian Removal Act
1831 Kinzie Party Arrival Big Foot Lake
1832 Black Hawk War
1833 Land Treaty With Native Americans Clears Southern Wisconsin Land Titles
1834 Refrigerator Invented
1834 Combine Harvester Invented
1835 John Brink Surveys And Renames Big Foot Lake
1835 Morse Code Invented
1836 Creation Of Wisconsin Territory
1836 Israel Williams Jr. Arrives On South Shore
1836 Wisconsin Territory Established
1836 Walworth County Organized Population 200
1836 Potawatomi Relocated To Kansas
1837 Israel Williams and Famly Arrive in Walworth County on July 4th
1837 Panic Of 1837, Banks Fail
1837 1841 Martin Van Buren
1838 Daguerreotype Photography Invented
1838 Electric Telegraph Invented
1838 Israel Williams Makes Claim In The Bay
1840 Israel Williams Builds Framed House
1840 Dam Built On White River Outlet
1840 Stage Coach Route Through Williams Bay
1841-Williams Henry Harrison
1841-1845 John Tyler
1842 Anesthesia Invented
1843 First Burial On Land Owned By Samuel Utter After The Accidental Death Of Alexander Utter; This Land Would Become East Delavan Union Cemetery
1844 First Blacksmith In The Bay
1844 Israel Williams First Postmaster Geneva Bay
1845 Typhoid Fever Outbreak
1845 Moses And Austin Williams, Sons Of Israel Williams Die From Typhoid Fever

1846-1849 James Polk
1846 Mexican-American War
1846 Rotary Printing Press Invented
1846 Israel Williams Dies Of Typhoid Fever
1847 Chloroform Invented
1848 Large Scale Immigration Of Germans And Norwegians Begins
1849 Kiah Bailey Postmaster Of Geneva Bay And Later Bay Hill
1849 1850 Zachary Taylor
1849 California Gold Rush
1850-1853 Millard Fillmore
1852 Lavina Joy Williams Dies
1853-1857 Franklin Pierce
1854 East Delavan Union Cemetery Formally Established
1854 Revolver Invented
1856-1860 Steam Train Chicago To Geneva
1857-1861 James Buchanan
1858 Heavy rainfall caused the Geneva Lake to be filled to full capacity in June
1858 First Steam Boat On Geneva Lake
1859 The Geneva Independents Militia Company Organized
1861-1865 Abraham Lincoln
1861-1865 American Civil War
1862 First Mechanical Submarine
1862 Company C Of The 22nd Wisconsin Infantry Formed
1864 Black Plague
1864 Pasteurization Process
1865-1869 Andrew Johnson
1866 Dynamite Invented
1867 Typewriter Invented
1869-1877 Ulysses S. Grant
1871 First Train Chicago To Geneva Arrived On Restored Railroad Line
1871 Great Chicago And Peshtigo Fires
1873 Camp Collie Opened
1873 First Lady Of The Lake Launched
1873 General U.S. Grant And Phillip Sheridan Summer On Geneva Lake
1873 Ice Boats Fist Appear On Geneva Lake
1873 Kaye's Park Opened
1873 Whiting House Opened

1874 First Large Commercial Ice House, Gross & Briggs, Geneva
1874 General Sherman And General Sheridan Visit Geneva Lake
1874 Lake Geneva Yacht Club Founded
1875 Steamer Lucius Newberry Built
1875 The First Sheridan Regatta
1876 Telephone Invented
1877-1881 Rutherford B. Hayes
1879 Light Bulb Invented
1880 Gramophone Invented
1880 Pishcotoqua Hotel Opened
1880 Telephone Line Around Geneva Lake Completed
1880 Three Passenger Trains And Two Freight Trains Arrive In Geneva Daily
1881- James Garfield
1881-1885 - Chester Arthur
1882 Congress Club
1883 19 Steamers On Geneva Lake
1883 The Lake Geneva Chapter Of The YMCA Founded
1884 Machine Gun Invented
1884 Steam Turbine Invented
1884 Lake Geneva Becomes A City
1885 Latter Day Saints Church Established At The Home Of Anthony Delap at Delap's Corner
1885 Construction Of Snake Road Completed
1885 Population Of Lake Geneva Is 2,281
1885 First Motorcycle
1885-1889 Grover Cleveland
1885 Oakwood Sanitarium Opened In Lake Geneva
1885 Hook And Ladder Fire Company Organized In Lake Geneva
1886 First Gas Powered Automobile
1886 Young Men's Christian Association Founded
1886 Royal Joy Williams Dies
1887 Holiday Home
1887 Wind Turbine For Grid Electricity
1888 Ball Point Pen Invented
1888 Chicago & North Western

U.S. AND GENEVA LAKE TIMELINE

Railroad Extended To Williams Bay

1888 Rockford Camp Founded

1889-1893 Benjamin Harrison

1889 Water, Street Lights, Waterworks, Water Tower, Fire Hydrants Installed In Lake Geneva

1890 Crane Farm Established

1890 21 Stream Yachts On Geneva Lake

1890 Telephone Line From Lake Geneva To Chicago Completed

1891 Geneva Lake Ice Co.

1891 Lake Geneva Railroad Depot Opened

1891 Scandinavian Free Lutheran Church Organized

1891 Steamer Lucius Newberry Destroyed By Fire

1892 Marie Williams Establishes Williams Bay Post Office

1891 Zipper Invented

1893-1897 Grover Cleveland

1893 World Columbian Exposition In Chicago

1893 Wireless Communication

1893 C.M. Williams Opens General Store

1893-1897 Financial Panic

1894 First U.S. Film - Fred Ott's Sneeze

1894 W. A. Lackey Establishes Livery Service

1894 Whiting House Hotel Burns

1895 H. G. Wells - Time Machine

1895 First Diesel Engine

1895 First Radio Signals

1895 L. E. Francis Establishes General Merchandise Store

1895 Lake Vista Hotel Opened

1895 Population Of Lake Geneva Is 2,452

1895 Charter Boat Dispatch Sinks In Storm Off Cedar Point—Six Lives Lost

1896 Congregation Church Organized

1897 Dr. Alice Bunker Stockham Opened New Thought School In Williams Bay

1897 J.P. Smith Ice Co.

1897 Yerkes Observatory Complete

1897-1901 Williams McKinley

1898 Remote Control Invented

1899 First School in Williams Bay

1900 Am Radio Invented

1900 Invention Of The Zeppelin

1901-1909 Theodore Roosevelt

1902 Kemah Farm

1902 Henry Ganzow Purchased Grocery Store From W. H. Howe

1903 First Motorized Aircraft Flies

1903 Gas Turbine

1903 Reverend George Chainey Opened Mahanaim School Of Interpretation

1906 Lake Geneva Yacht Club Moved To Cedar Point

1907 Bakelite Invented

1906 Williams Bay Library Established By Storrs B. Barrett

1907 Radio Amplifier

1907 Anna Peterson Named Williams Bay Postmaster

1908 Festus Allen Williams Dies

1909 Olivet Camp

1909-1913 Williams Taft

1911 Congregation Church Burns

1912 Congregational Church Rebuilt

1913-1921 Woodrow Wilson

1915 Williams Bay Joint District 1 - New Brick School Built

1914-1918 World War I

1919 Village Of Williams Bay Incorporated; Population Is 492

1920-1923 Prohibition

1921-1923 Warren Harding

1920 Geneva Lake Water Safety Patrol Established

1922 Old Williams Bay School Burns Down

1921 Loch Vista Subdivision

1922 Williams Bay Village Board Contracts Jacob Crane To Develop The First Village Master Plan

1923-1929 Calvin Coolidge

1923 Astronomer E. E. Barnard Dies At His Home In Williams Bay

1923 Lackey Brothers Subdivision

1924 Jewell Subdivision

1923 First Sound Film

1923 Invention of Electro Mechanical Television System

1925 Cedar Point Park Subdivision Founded

1927 Quartz Clock Invented

1927 First Williams Bay Women's Banquet Held At Rose Lane Lodge

1927 Geneva Lake Historical Society Formed At Yerkes Observatory

1928 First Antibiotics

1929-1933 Herbert Hoover

1929 Stock Market Crash

1929-1939 The Great Depression

1929 Williams Bay Develops Edgewater Park

1930 Williams Bay Population Is 630

1930 Williams Bay Garden Club Established

1931 Geneva Lake Centennial Celebration

1931 Iconoscope Invented

1933-1934 Century Of Progress, Chicago

1933-1945 Franklin D. Roosevelt

1933 The Hollyhock Is Named The Official Flower Of Williams Bay By The Garden Club

1933 Invention Of The Fm Radio

1935 Astronomer Edwin. B. Frost Dies

1935 Frost Park Dedicated

1937 First Jet Engine

1937 First Village President And Astronomer Storrs B. Barrett Dies

1939 Williams Bay Purchases Lakefront Property From Chicago & North Western Railway

1939 Germany Invades Poland

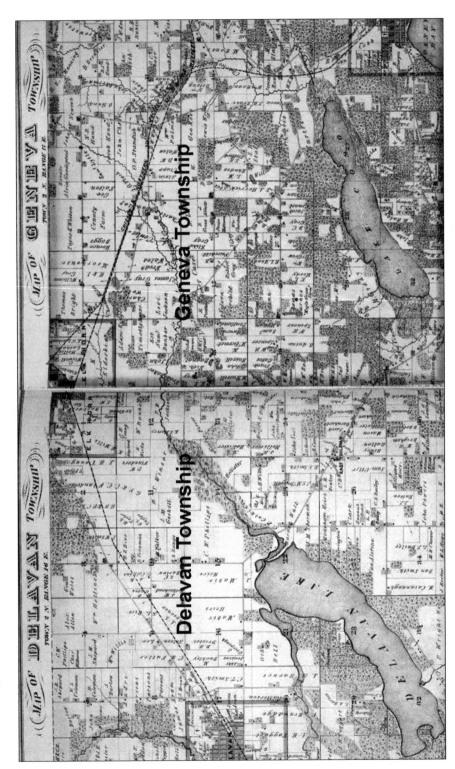

Delavan Township

Geneva Township

iv

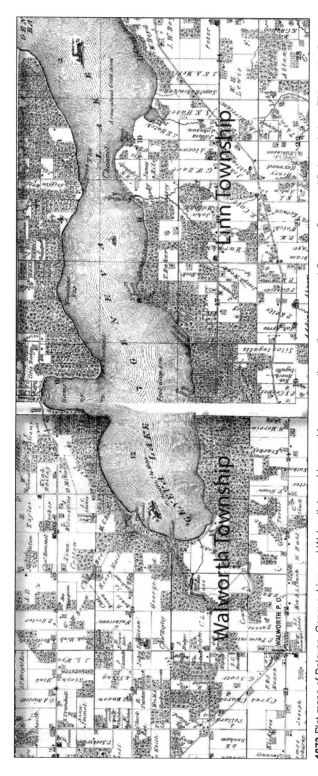

1873 Plat maps of Delavan, Geneva, Linn, and Walworth townships provide a perspective on the area around Geneva, Como and Delavan Lakes. Elkhorn, the County seat is shown on the upper portion of the Delavan and Geneva maps. The maps also provide the names of land owners where the four corners of the townships intersected north of Williams Bay. Photo credit: Deborah Dumelle Kristmann and Michelle Bie Love.

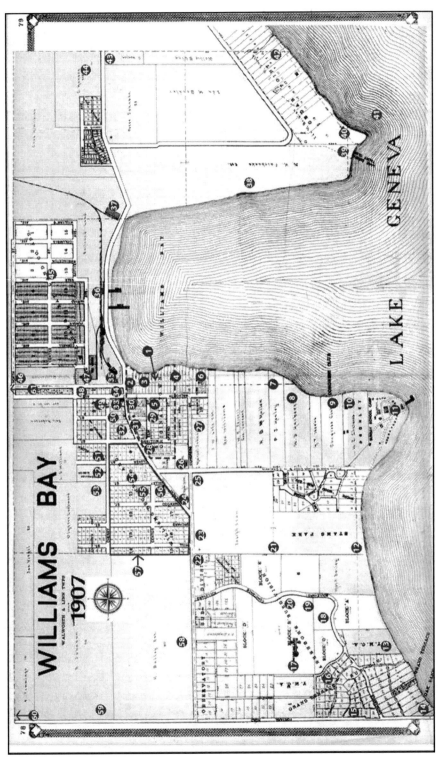

WILLIAMS BAY
WALWORTH & LINN TWP.
1907

LAKE GENEVA

MAP LEGEND

1. Boundary area of the original part of the Village
2. Edward Williams home, location of first Williams Bay post office; Hansen livery; 1936 Fire Station
3. Bay Shore Inn
4. Resorts: Normandie Hotel; Twin Cottages; Rose Lane Lodge; Sawyer's Cottages
5. Fernwood Inn later Clarendell Hotel
6. Mahanaim School of Interpretation; Ferndale Inn
7. P. J. Healey estate
8. Tre-brah estate of William and Elizabeth Harbert
9. Congress Club
10. Dronley estate of William and Joan Chalmers
11. Camp Collie; Sunday School Camp; Conference Point
12. Eleanor Camp
13. YMCA Camp; George Williams College Camp
14. Alice B. Stockham's Vralia Heights; Olivet Camp; Norman B. Barr Camp
15. Vision Hill
16. E. E. Barnard residence
17. Yerkes Observatory
18. Observatory Director's house
19. Morgan House
20. Observatory Powerhouse.
21. Brantwood - Edwin B. Frost residence
22. Zebulon Sawyer residence and greenhouse
23. Joseph Stam

24. Edwin B. Frost Park
25. Williams Bay School 1915-2016
26. Williams Bay School 1900-1915
27. Michael Johnson discovers mastodon bones and teeth in his garden on Congress Street in 1907
28. Scandinavian Free Church; first school; Gospel Tabernacle; Calvary Community Church
29. Sacred Potawatomi burial ground
30. Livery barn, Hopkins and Walker garage.
31. Israel Williams homestead and barn; Buck Horn Tavern; Library
32. Southwick Merchantile; Dr. Fucik office
33. Lake Vista Hotel; Lackey Building
34. W. G. DeGroff residence; location of post office in 1898
35. Lackey Lumber and Coal; Hollister Lumberyard
36. Chicago & North Western Depot
37. Smith Ice House
38. Fairbank's woods; Cedar Point
39. Lake Geneva Yacht Club
40. Lawn Glen estate of Edward B. Meatyard; Alpine Villa estate of Herbert A. Beidler
41. Steamer Dispatch sinks off Cedar Point in 108 feet of water; 6 lives lost on July 7, 1895
42. Trawley estate of John M. Smyth
43. Hansen homestead
44. Otis Dodge farm

45. Williams Bay Land Company
46. Celery Farm
47. Knickerbocker Ice House
48. Blacksmith shop
49. Johnson bike rental
50. Solid Comfort Resort
51. Rest Cottage Resort
52. Sherwood Resort
53. Johnson Dairy
54. Pihl Lumberyard
55. Truck farm
56. Congregational Church
57. Williams Second Addition platted 1889
58. Kiah Bailey cabin; Bay Hill post office
59. Lake Lane Farm
60. To East Delavan Union Cemetery and East Delavan
61. To DeLap's Corner

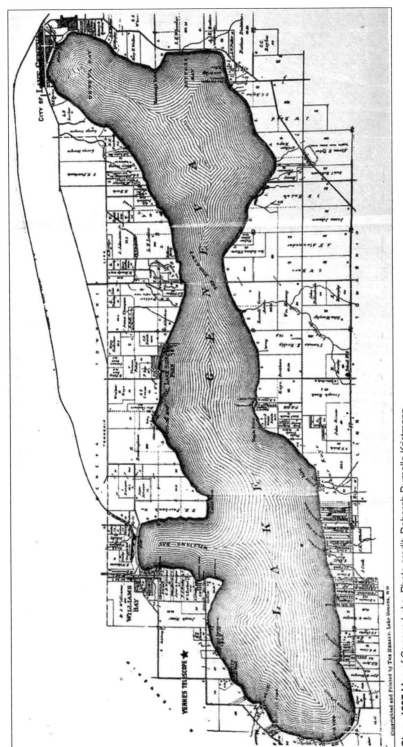

Circa **1897** Map of Geneva Lake. Photo credit: Deborah Dumelle Kristmann.

ODE TO WILLIAMS BAY

On your sparkling clear
Kishwauketoe shores
peaceful
native Potawatomi
lived, loved
foraged and thrived
on the generous
harvest of your lake
and surrounding
fertile fields
where burial mounds
still silently mark
their place of rest.

Born hugging the
majestic lake
in your arms
and named for your
first white settlers
you blossomed into
our fair Village
of Williams Bay.
After the turn of two centuries
you are alive with
historic memories.

Vibrant
and early active
you proudly boasted
a thriving railroad
houses of worship
summer stock theater
and Edgewater cinemas
carnivals and concerts.
Campuses and an
extravagance of lush
verdant conservancy
now enhance
your eclectic charm.

Transported across
the lake's winter ice
your first cottage
library arrived on
your frozen shores with
grateful thanks to
Storrs B. Barrett
—library namesake
astronomer
and early resident
whose grandson's
family still occupies
their once shared home.

Your Yerkes Observatory
proudly wears
its stately dome
like a crown
resting on the brow
of your beautiful bay
as a tribute in
loving memory of its
renowned astronomers.

Bountifully blessed with
charitable organizations
excellent schools
and the everyday joy
of resort living
—your caring families
continue to make you a
friendly small village
with a large heart.

Williams Bay
you are life and
sanctuary to we
who choose to abide
in your comfortable
cozy corner of the world.

Guri Henderson 2010

PREFACE

A Pictorial History of Williams Bay on Beautiful Geneva Lake is largely a compilation of previously published information organized for a modern reader. The following pages draw from these earlier works giving context to the influence of the U.S. social movements on the settlement, growth, and development of the Village of Williams Bay. Much is owed to those who have documented the earliest recollections and history of the Geneva Lake area:

Juliette Kinzie's *Wau-Bun The Early Day in the Northwest* (1857), James Simmons' *History of Geneva, Wisconsin* (1875), Western Historical Company's *History of Walworth County, Wisconsin* (1882), William C. Dean's the *Williams Bay Observer (1896-97)*, James Simmons' *Annals of Lake Geneva 1835-1897* (1897), George E. Hale's *The Yerkes Observatory of the University of Chicago* (1897), *Lovely Lake Geneva and its Noble Charity*, National Magazine (1905), Albert Clayton Beckwith's *History of Walworth County, Wisconsin* (1912), Edwin B. Frost's *Yerkes Observatory* (1914), Paul B. Jenkins' *The Book of Lake Geneva* (1922), Paul B. Jenkins and Charles E. Brown's, *History and Indian Remains of Lake Geneva and Lake Como* (1930), Frank Van Epps' *Bay Leaves (1933-1941 and 1946-1954)*, Larry Larkin's *Full Speed Ahead* (1972), and Maggie Gage and Ann Wolfmeyer's, *Lake Geneva - Newport of the West 1870-1920* (1976), Phil Fogle's *Grassroots-- Lake Geneva: An illustrated history of the Geneva Lake area* (1986).

Special note to the Reader: Geneva Lake (the lake itself) has been known by many names; the first "white" settlers knew it as *Big Foot*, the Potawatomi called it *Kishwauketoe* (meaning Clearwater), and surveyor John Brink renamed the lake *Geneva* in 1835. At some point in time, it was clarified that "Geneva Lake" is the name of the lake, while "Lake Geneva" is the name of the city located on the eastern shore of the lake.

Early maps of the Geneva Lake area from the 1850s show what is now known as Williams Bay as Geneva Bay. The first post office in 1844 was known as Geneva Bay and was run by its first settler Captain Israel Williams. Later, the bay on which the City of Lake Geneva is located became known as Geneva Bay (as it remains today) and what had been called Geneva Bay was named Williams Bay.

Every effort has been made to provide accurate information, any errors and/or discrepancies can be addressed directly by contacting the Williams Bay Historical Society.

Email wmsbayhistoricalsociety@gmail.com

INTRODUCTION
HISTORY OF THE AREA
1836 -1939

The beautiful Geneva Lake area of Walworth County in southeastern Wisconsin is probably best known for the many resorts, summer camps and residences that dot its shoreline. Year-round recreation and leisure activities draw hundreds of thousands annually for rest and recreation. The City of Lake Geneva, on the far eastern shore or the foot of Geneva Lake, on the outlet of the White River, is the largest and oldest of three communities on the lake. Fontana-on-the-Lake is located to the west at what is known as the head of the lake and on

the northern shore, at the lake's widest point, is the Village of Williams Bay. While these quaint communities have much history in common, this book focuses on the unique history of the Village of Williams Bay. Its story illustrates on a smaller scale the spirit and growth of the United States at a time when the Northwest Territory (pre-Revolutionary War territory of the Ohio Country, parts of Illinois

Map of the Northern Parts of Ohio, Indiana and Illinois with Michigan and That Part of the Ouisconsin Territory Lying East of the Mississippi River. U.S. House Report 380. Washington, DC: Blair & Rives, printers, 1836. Photo credit: Michigan State University.[1]

Country, and parts of old French Canada below the Great Lakes) was largely unexplored and unknown. Our young country beckoned its citizens to the western frontier, where land ownership, farming, independence, upward mobility, and opportunities seemed endless. Pioneers and immigrants came in droves to settle in the region. They worked hard and built a thriving village anchored by its citizens' strong sense of community and contribution.

As the turn of the 20th century approached, the small Village of Williams Bay did more than thrive: it was known worldwide as the home of Yerkes Observatory and its great 40-inch refractor telescope, the most technologically advanced mechanism of its kind and the birthplace of modern astrophysics. This magnificent new telescope stood on display at the 1893 World Columbian Exposition where patrons looked up in awe at its size and wondered of the heavens and possibilities never before imagined.

Conveniently located near the growing industrial cities of Racine, Milwaukee, and Chicago and accessible by the Chicago & North Western railway the Geneva Lake area and Williams Bay quickly grew into a recreational and resort community in the backyard of these bustling cities.

Big Foot - Home of the Potawatomi

Mural by Louis Grell commissioned by the Northwest Military Academy Class of 1939 depicting the Potawatomi prior to white settlement of the area. Photo credit: Dwight Heats Photography and the Louis Grell family.

At the time of the Potawatomi habitation, Geneva Lake was known by the "white man" as "Big Foot" after the name of their chief. The Potawatomi people knew the lake as Kishwauketoe, meaning "clear water." The name Potawatomi means "keepers of the fire" or "those who keep the council-fire going." The council-fire refers to the place around which peace proposals were made and agreed to. The Potawatomi have always been a peaceful people. The Potawatomi of Geneva Lake originated in central New York where they were part of the Algonkian (Algonquin) tribe. Their community was a more peaceful band, it is likely they fled west due to warfare waged by more aggressive neighboring tribes.

Sometime during the 18th century, the Potawatomi people settled on the shore of the lake we now know as Geneva abundant land with natural resources: game, fur-bearing animals, fish, waterfowl, plant life, and fertile land for growing corn, beans, squash, and tobacco. Hardwood maples produced coarse sugar, roots and tubers were harvested from the marshes and swamps, nuts, wild plums, berries, grapes, and cherries were plentiful, and reeds and grasses from the marshes were woven into grass mats. As was common with other forest dwellers, the Potawatomi rarely used the "teepee," but instead lived in semi- permanent lodges called wigwams; a rounded hut, with grass and reed mats used for the sides and large slabs of bark from whole trees for the roof.

The Potawatomi lived at three locations along the lake's shores: at the head of the lake in what is now Fontana, near the northwest corner of the lake's northern bay in what is now Williams Bay and at the foot of the lake at its eastern point that is now the City of Lake Geneva. The camp in Williams Bay was one of the favorite camps of Chief Big Foot, who had his main or royal residence and council pole in Fontana. A well-defined trail followed the banks of the lake between Big Foot's camps and other trails that led to favorite camping, hunting and fishing spots.[2]

Wisconsin Indian Trails Map fousing on Southeast Wisconsin. Wisconsin Archeological Society, Charles E. Brown, 1930. Photo credit: Wisconsin State Historical Society.

One might wonder what the "white man" knew about Kishwauketoe Lake and the Potawatomi people before the arrival of the Kinzie party in 1831. Well-worn trails crisscrossed the landscape of the Northwest Territory, leading to and from native settlements, hunting grounds, camp sites, and the newly established American settlements of Fort Dearborn (Chicago),

3

Milwaukee, and Racine. According to *History and Indian Remains of Lake Geneva and Lake Como*, "It is likely that French fur traders were the first to come upon the lake, however no factual recorded information has ever been found." Coins dating up to thirty years prior to the first known visit of the white man to Geneva Lake have been found along its shores. These coins may have been lost by early traders or may have been in the possession of the Potawatomi people who obtained them in trade and dropped them. One thing that does seem clear is that the existence of Geneva Lake and the Potawatomi living on its shores was known to the whites before any recorded visit. The local Potawatomi were accustomed to bringing goods for trade to the Kinzie post at Fort Dearborn.

According to *The Book of Lake Geneva*, "The white pioneers who first traveled to southeastern Wisconsin were very fortunate of the generally peaceful character of the Potawatomi who had already encountered and begun trading with white men. At this point in time, the natives were just becoming aware of the irresistible tide of the westward migration of the American settlement."

As a result of the Winnebago war scare of 1827 and the Black Hawk War in 1832, the military presence had increased on the frontier with the building Fort Winnebago and reoccupying of two other abandoned forts. Many were convinced that settlers and "Indians" could not live peaceably together, and that the Indians should be forced to move westward, a policy known as the Indian Removal Act, signed on May 28, 1830, that resulted in the "Trail of Tears."

The westward expansion of the United States is one of the defining themes of 19th-century American history. When Andrew Jackson took office in 1829, 125,000 Native Americans still lived east of the Mississippi River. The key political issue of the time was whether these Native American people would be permitted to block white expansion and whether the U.S. government would abide by previous treaties. Jackson's policy was to encourage Native Americans to sell their homelands in exchange for new lands in Kansas, Oklahoma, and Arkansas. This would open new farmland to settlers while offering Native Americans a haven where they would be free to develop at their own pace. In reality, the Natives Americans were given barren, flat, dry land that was ill suited for farming.

4

KINZIE PARTY - DISCOVERY OF BIG FOOT AND SETTLEMENT

Mural by Louis Grell commissioned by the Northwest Military Academy Class of 1940 depicting the arrival of the Kinzie Party at Big Foot Lake. Photo credit: Dwight Heats Photography and the Louis Grell Family.

John Harris Kinzie
Photo credit:
Chicago Historical
Society.

The first documented white men to view the lake and Chief Big Foot's camp occurred in the spring of 1831. John H. Kinzie, the U.S. sub-Indian Agent (in the 1830s, Indian agents assisted in commercial trading between traders and Indians) and son of the famous fur trader John Kinzie at Fort Dearborn, was traveling from Fort Dearborn to Fort Winnebago on a known but untraveled Indian trail via "Big-Foot Lake."[3] During this trip, they became the first known white people to visit the shores of Big Foot (later renamed Geneva Lake).

Mrs. Juliette Kinzie
Photo credit:
Chicago Historical
Society.

The party consisted of Mr. Kinzie and his wife, Juliette; his mother, Mrs. John Kinzie; a sister, Mrs. LT. Helm; her little boy, Edwin; two French employees, Petaille Gringon and Simon Lecuyer; a young half-breed "bound-girl," Josette Ouilmette, the daughter of a Frenchman and his Potawatomi squaw (the father's name perpetuated today as Wilmette, the northern suburb of Chicago); and a Negro boy, Harry, formerly a slave but now, with Illinois becoming "free territory," a legal ward of Mr. Kinzie. The men and the younger Mrs. Kinzie and Mrs. Helm traveled on horseback, the others riding in a light "Dearborn wagon" brought from Detroit "the first luxury of the kind ever seen on the prairie," as Mrs. Kinzie described it. Shortly after noon on the fourth day of the trip, the party first caught sight of Geneva Lake. It seems evident from the way Mrs. Kinzie spoke of the lake as one of their intended stops that they knew of its existence and location, and others of the time must have known of it as well. Her striking description of the arrival of the party draws a vivid picture: "Soon after mid-day, we descended a long, sloping knoll, and by a sudden turn came full in view of the beautiful sheet of water denominated Gros-pied by the French, in the Potawatomi tongue "Kishwauketoe," or "Clear Water," by which it was known to the tribes of the Middle West, and by ourselves Big-foot, from the Chief whose village overlooked its waters. Bold, swelling hills jutted forward into the clear blue expanse, or retreated slightly to afford a green, level nook, as a resting place for the dwelling of man. On the nearer shore stretched a bright, gravelly beach, across which coursed here and there a pure, sparkling rivulet to join the larger sheet of water. On a rising ground at the foot of one of the bold bluffs in the middle distance, a collection of neat wigwams formed, with their surrounding gardens, no unpleasant feature in the picture."[4]

Juliette Kinzie's drawing of Big Foot Lake and Chief Big Foot's village (location of Buena Vista at Fontana) as it appeared in 1831. Photo credit: *Wau-bun the 'Early Day' in the Northwest* by Juliette Augusta Magill Kinzie, 1856.

WESTWARD EXPANSION

Westward expansion was the political and social theme that had the newly formed United States and its citizens abuzz. There was a contagious widespread national spirit of adventure as settlers and frontiersmen pushed westward, where rich and fertile lands were abundant and natural resources flourished. Rich gains and profits could be made in business by supplying the needs of newly settled

communities. Pioneers and immigrants were on the move. Army posts were established throughout the American west, sometimes to keep the native tribes from waging war with each other and at other times to protect white settlers from attack. As more posts were built, one chief grew angry. Chief Black Hawk of the Sauk nation formed an alliance of local tribes that took a last stand against the encroaching white man. The conflict took place in 1832 and Black Hawk's band of 500-plus warriors were outnumbered by more

Chief Black Hawk Photo credit: History of the Indian Tribes of North America.

than 6,000 militiamen. Black Hawk's defeat became the pinnacle to opening the new territory for settlement west to the Mississippi. Native Americans were pushed further west to Iowa and Kansas, eliminating the danger of further "savage hostilities" resulting in the rapid settlement of the fertile lands in the little-known "frontier" territory of southern Wisconsin.

TREATY OF 1833 - POTAWATOMI LEAVE BIG FOOT LAKE

On the afternoon of September 21, 1833, several thousand braves and their families, dressed in their finest were encamped on every available spot at the mouth of the river surrounding Fort Dearborn. Chief Big Foot was one of the 20 to 30 chieftains representing the various tribes of the Potawatomi people who spent several days negotiating with representatives of the federal government at a meeting of the Grand Council. As a result, Chief Big Foot promised to give up the land on which his tribe lived on and around Big Foot Lake. In total the Chippewa, Ottawa, and Potawatomi in conjunction with the recently signed treaties of the Winnebago Nation (treaty of Ft. Armstrong) and the Menomonees (treaty of Prairie du Chien) gave up about 5 million acres within three years in exchange for an equal amount of land in Kansas. The federal government agreed to transport them, pay all costs for the trip, and to support them for one year after their arrival. The final scene at the Grand Council was a great "war dance" in which approximately 800 took part.

It is estimated that there were some five hundred Potawatomi living around Geneva Lake when they left by wagon for Kansas in the fall of 1836. Before leaving for this long journey west, Chief Big Foot visited the burial place of his wives and children at Williams Bay (it has been speculated that their deaths were caused by whooping cough [pertussis] that had affected the area at the time of their departure). Each body was adorned in decorative costume and supplied with a tin pail filled with whiskey, a pipe, and some food for their journey into the spirit world. Over all was a tent-like covering of bark. Likewise, Chief Big Foot placed his arm around the Council Pole at Fontana and took a long last look at the lake and the coffin of his son in the treetop overlooking the fishing grounds. Then after stopping for a word of farewell with Mrs. Catherine Van Slyke (the

Van Slykes were the first residents of Fontana), and commending the care of the treetop grave to her, he followed his tribe over the hills toward the long trail to Kansas, never again to see Geneva Lake.[5]

SURVEYOR JOHN BRINK - OPEN TERRITORY

Government surveyor John Brink who came to the Wisconsin Territory to survey Walworth County in 1835. Photo credit: Crystal Lake Historical Society.

Surveyors John Brink and John Hodgson came to the territory in 1835 to survey section lines in what would become Walworth County. Contrary to instructions to use the Native American names for lakes, John Brink changed the name of Kishwauketoe Lake to Geneva Lake after his beloved home in New York State. Surveying for section lines in Walworth County was completed in 1836 opening land in the county for settlement. Early settlers of Williams Bay did not leave much in writing about their experiences. However, Colonel Samuel F. Phoenix, the first settler in Delavan, kept a diary that described the area.

"To the early explorers the county seemed a veritable paradise, waiting only for man to enter into possession. The southern and eastern parts of the county, which were the first to be viewed by prospectors, was watered by the most considerable lakes in the county. Geneva Lake stretched for nine miles through heavily wooded rolling country, opening out at its southern extremity onto the beautiful prairie of Big Foot. Across the county, some three miles to the northwest, another beautiful lake, then known as Swan Lake (Delavan Lake) lay in all its native loveliness, quite heavily wooded about its banks but flanked farther north by open prairie and groves, or openings as they were termed, of oaks. The oaks had a peculiar fascination for the incoming explorers. Few of them had ever seen the like before. Emerging from the deep woods, they came upon these natural parks, as clear of underbrush as an ordinary orchard,

Survey map of Township 1 North Range 17 East Government surveyor John Brink. Photo credit: Board of Commissioners of Public Lands.

and skirting the prairies on every side." The first farmers staked their claims along borders of these openings generally including a strip of timber in which to build a house and barn and a strip of prairie to farm.

By the summer of 1836, settlements had sprung up in Spring Prairie, Geneva, East Troy, Troy, and Delavan, though they were known by the names of the settlement's principal families: Hemenway, Warren, McCracken, Meacham, and Phoenix, respectively. By the end of 1836, 27 families (two hundred men, women, and children) were living in what is now Walworth County. By 1840, the population in Walworth County was 2,611. In 1848, Wisconsin became the 30th state in the Union and in 1850, the population in Walworth County rose to 17,862.

ENTICEMENT OF SETTLERS AND IMMIGRANTS TO WISCONSIN

Early image of drying corn shocks in the fields of Walworth County. Photo credit: Paul B. Jenkins, *The Book of Lake Geneva.*

The population of Wisconsin was growing exponentially as abundant fertile land was open to be claimed. Between 1836 and 1850, Wisconsin's population increased from 11,000 to over 305,000. Of this number, one-third were foreign born. Easterners from the coast came to farm virgin land and seek out new opportunities, while Europeans were motivated by opportunities for upward mobility and political struggles in their homelands. Germans and Norwegians constituted the largest groups to emigrate.

They came by ship, by steamboat, by railroad, on horseback, and in wagons. Milwaukee became a favorite landing place for lake passengers because of its expanding business opportunities and public lands office. Between 1852 and 1855, the Wisconsin Commission of Emigration actively encouraged the settlement of European immigrants in Wisconsin. Pamphlets extolling the state's virtues were published in German, Norwegian, Dutch, and English and were distributed throughout Europe as well as in eastern port cities. Advertisements were placed in more than nine-hundred newspapers. By 1855, however, the rise of anti-foreign sentiment led to the dissolution of the commission.[6,7,8]

ISRAEL WILLIAMS FAMILY–THE EARLIEST SETTLERS IN THE BAY

Captain Israel Williams, his wife Lavina Joy (b. 1787, d. 1852) and their nine children are noted to be the first settlers of Williams Bay, Wisconsin. They originated from Ashfield, Massachusetts.

Israel's grandfather, Daniel owned a saw mill in Easton Massachusetts and was a non-resident land owner in Huntstown Plantation, which incorporated as Ashfield in June 1765. Daniel's wife, Rebecca Hunt, was the granddaughter of Captain Ephraim Hunt, for whom the town was first named. This land was given by the General Court in 1736 to the Weymouth soldiers, their heirs or assigns, who had accompanied Ephraim Hunt to Canada in 1692. Daniel Williams had acquired over 300 acres in Huntstown by 1766, mostly from his wife's relatives. Thus he became a Huntstown Proprietor. He visited Huntstown in 1769 to 1770, and was encouraged to build a saw mill in 1769 at what is now the Spruce Corner School District. Daniel's son, Ephraim, may

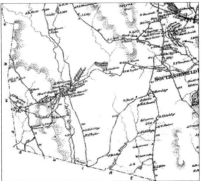

Circa 1760s Map of Ashfield, Massachusetts. Spruce Corners and the Swift River is located on the lower left side of the map. Photo credit: Maps of Antiquity.

have built the mill beginning in 1771. In 1775 Ephraim married Mercy Daniels of Mendon and they settled permanently next to the saw mill "on ye Brook," a tributary of the Swift River in Spruce Corners.

Israel Williams was probably a member of either the Ashfield North or South Companies of the State militia. Contrary to a long held belief, Israel Williams did not serve in the War of 1812. In 1814 Ashfield sent nine men from these two militia companies to serve in the Boston area, but Israel was not one of those chosen.[8] In 1820, Israel Williams was elected to the position of Lieutenant of a Company in the 5th Regiment of Infantry in the 2nd Brigade and 4th Division of the Militia of the Commonwealth of Massachusetts. In 1825, he was elected to the position of Captain in the same Brigade.[9,10]

Israel married Lavina Joy in 1808 in Plainfield, Massachusetts. Lavina was the daughter of Nehemiah and Hannah (Leach) Joy. Nehemiah Joy, a Revolutionary War soldier, died in May 1830 and was buried in Hill Cemetery, Ashfield. Hannah Joy accompanied Israel and Lavina to Wisconsin in 1837.

Of the children, the two older sons, Moses and Israel Jr., were grown men and married. The other children were Royal, Austin, Francis, Fordyce, Festus, Hannah, and Lavina. Though settled into a prosperous life in Ashfield, Captain Williams and the two older sons and their wives sold much of their land in anticipation of seeking a new home in the vast Midwest which had just been opened for settlement in 1836. Israel Williams' family went to Wisconsin about the same time as their neighbors, Oliver Rawson (as Renson) and his wife, Lois Howes. The Rawson's son-in-law, Elihu Higgins, had moved there earlier. Granville B. Hall had a claim to land (#2075) in Walworth County, Wisconsin. He stayed on the claim to satisfy the residency requirements, but then returned to Ashfield.

Captain Williams, his two oldest sons, and their wives Eliza and Lucinda, went as far as Michigan. Israel Jr. and Moses continued on to investigate the country in Southeastern Wisconsin around "Big Foot Lake," which they had heard of during their stay in Michigan. With rifle and ax in hand, they reached the south shore of the lake where each proceeded to establish a "claim" by erecting a crude log cabin. The first of these was on land claimed by Israel Jr that later became known as Kaye's Park, Northwestern Military and Naval Academy, and presently the South Shore Club. On completion of the first cabin they built a second cabin farther west for Moses at Nine Oaks, which later became the Edward Ayer estate and is now Abbey Springs. At about this time, Israel Jr. and Moses became neighbors and close friends with Mark and Robert Russell, young men from a Shaker settlement in Ohio.

Once their cabins were completed, Israel Jr. and Moses returned to Michigan for their wives, and on receiving their report, Captain Williams returned to Massachusetts for the remainder of the family. The sons and their wives returned to Geneva Lake spending the winter of 1836 -1837 in their new homes on the south shore. Moses also made a land claim in Walworth Township for his brother Royal.

Royal (aged 18) and Austin (aged 16) joined their older brothers in August of 1836, landing at Milwaukee and successfully making their way on foot through the wilderness to Geneva Lake.

The Potawatomi were still living in their villages though they were to be removed the fall of 1836 and sent to Kansas. It must have been at this time that the original above ground "burial" of two of Chief Big Foot's wives were placed in Williams Bay. The two must have succumbed to whooping cough (pertussis) which had affected the area shortly before their departure. After the Potawatomi left it is almost certain that these remains were interred on the spot by the Williams family (the only settlers in the area at the time) who by custom would have likely preferred to have them underground. Festus Williams witnessed the burial as a young boy and later in 1890 recounted the event to author James Simmons, Annals of Lake Geneva. In 1920, Mr. Edward H. Hollister, who owned the neighboring residence, excavated the mound which was the known location of the grave. He unearthed the skeleton of one of the women, while Mrs. Hollister carefully sifted out of the earth uncovering numerous burial ornaments; fragments of decorative silver disks, tiny bells, finger rings, earrings, and beads (both "trade" and native origin).[11] It was

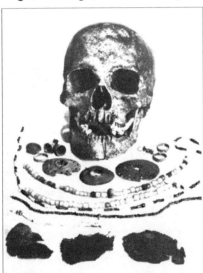

clear these artifacts matched the description of Festus Williams to James Simmons 30 years earlier, however only one adult skull was found. In the same grave, were the skeletons of two small children, a small dog (possibly a pet killed and buried with them to be their companion in the spirit world) and several bones of fowls (perhaps prairie chickens) thought to be part of the food placed with the remains.[12]

Artifacts excavated by Edward Hollister from the Sacred Burial Grounds on Elm Street. Photo credit: *The Book of Lake Geneva*, Paul B. Jenkins.

As the weather warmed in the spring of 1837, there was a constant stream of new settlers to the county. Traveling by sailing schooner through the Great Lakes and probably landing at Chicago-for which there is some evidence in letters written by Captain Israel Williams, his wife Lavina, Mrs. Hannah Joy, mother of Lavina, and the rest of the children reached the lake on July 4, 1837. One son, Frances, at college in Massachusetts, remained behind to complete his studies, later joining the others, but eventually returning to the east where he became a Congregational minister at Chaplin, Connecticut.

In 1837, a newcomer named Cole had noted the low, fertile land on the north and northwest shores of the principal bay now Williams Bay - where the old Indian village had been vacated the year before. Contemplating a claim there, he staked out lots destined for future sale, but failed to comply with the simple government stipulation that a man wishing to stake a claim had to hew off the bark from a tree and inscribe his name in red chalk on the tree. He was then allowed thirty days to begin improvements; at the end of that time if nothing had been done toward building a house his claim was forfeited. For some reason Mr. Cole failed to begin improvements and Captain Williams who saw the desirability of the location, decided to "jump" the claim.

Captain Williams, recognizing the potential of the abandoned claim, lost no time in claiming it as his own, and with his five older sons and Robert Russell began to build a log cabin on the site. Cole, learning of this "jumping" of his desired site, returned with three companions, all armed, and ordered the Williams party off the property.

Captain Williams' group of six promptly exchanged their axes for their guns and announced their intentions of staying. Before their leveled muzzles, Cole and his group decided that they didn't stand a chance: land laws were against them and they were also outnumbered.

Discretion was the bet-

Artist rendering of the standoff between Captain Williams and Cole. Photo credit: *The Yankee Pioneers of Williams Bay*, The Milwaukee Journal, June 11, 1927.

ter part of valor, and they left accordingly. Later Captain Williams gave Cole a cow as an amicable settlement.

In the spring of 1838, Captain Williams brought the members of his household to the new cabin beside the bay and planted his first crops on the old Indian gardens. The nearest post office at this time was Racine, from which most of the necessary supplies were purchased. Over a hundred acres of today's village consisted only of water, swamp, and marsh. When the land came onto the market, Captain Williams purchased large tracts of land in Linn, Walworth, and Delavan townships. He also purchased a number of cows and established a dairy which produced enough milk to enable Lavina to produce 800 pounds of cheese in 1839. This was the first cheese made in Walworth County and was delivered to the settlement in Geneva by canoe and sold to Andrew Ferguson.

Wisconsin farm wives made "kitchen" cheese from milk produced by their herds. Photo credit: Wisconsin Milk Marketing Board.

In 1838, Robert Russell married Hannah Williams. The ceremony took place in the home of her brother Israel Jr., the newly appointed Justice of the Peace in Linn township.[13] Later accounts have erroneously stated Captain Israel Williams was Justice of the Peace.

Early in the fall of 1838, Mrs. Hannah Joy, mother of Lavina Williams, who had accompanied the family from their home in Ashfield, Massachusetts, died at the Williams cabin. Squire Bell of Big Foot Prairie gave a prayer and she was interred in a home-made basswood coffin near the remains of Chief Big Foot's wives on what is now Elm Street. Later in 1892, Festus Williams had his grandmother's remains moved to East Delavan Cemetery.

Mrs. Moses Williams taught the first school in 1839 at their home at Nine Oaks on the south shore of the lake. Her pupils were Festus Williams, three of James Van Slyke's children, two of Squire Bell's children, two of Doctor Woods' children, and two of Mr. Clark's. The Woods and Clark families were recent settlers on the south shore. Mrs. Williams taught school at the Van Slyke residence in 1840 and also at the Robert Russell home at the head of the lake for two terms.

In the fall and winter of 1839-1840 Captain Williams, assisted by his sons and Mark Russell, began hewing the timbers to build what was, for the time, a very large frame house, the "Old Williams House" (near current the Bay View Motel) and a barn. Much of the timber used in its construction was highly desirable black walnut. Neighbors came from miles to attend the raising which was a grand affair. Upon completion in 1840, a large rack of deer antlers were placed over the entry and the place became known as "Williams' Buck-Horn Hotel," which contained a tavern and a headquarters for land seekers of the lake country. It was also a stagecoach stop on the line connecting "Southport" (now Kenosha) and Beloit. This road continued over the grounds of what would later become Yerkes Observatory. Here it followed the undoubtedly ancient overland Indian trail or shortcut between the east end of the lake and the head of the bay, a path known to the first whites as the "Army Trail," from its use by troops moving between old Fort Dearborn and points northward, to Fort Howard at Green Bay.

During the early years in the west, illness was rampant among settlers, as evidenced by the early headstones in local cemeteries. Children were especially susceptible to illness and suffered a high mortality rate. Moses and Austin Williams, sons of Israel Williams Sr., became ill with typhoid fever in September 1845 and died within three days of each other. Captain Williams succumbed to the same disease on October 14, 1846. After the death of Captain Williams, Mrs. Lavina Williams and son Festus moved to Broom Prairie (Spring Prairie) to live with Israel Jr. and his family who had moved there some time earlier. Their stay was short lived; they returned to the family homestead in Williams Bay in 1848 due to disagreements Lavina had with her daughter-in-law, Eliza.[14]

Royal had returned to Massachusetts in 1844, but returned to Wisconsin after Mrs. Williams' death in June 1852, and was appointed administrator of the estate. Members of the Williams family continued to live in the family homestead until the death of Royal's son George in 1924.[15,16] Israel Williams Jr. ventured west during the Gold Rush.[17]

EARLY SETTLERS AND DEVELOPMENT OF THE BAY

The first post offices in Walworth County were established in Delavan, Elkhorn, and Troy in about 1837. There were 13 post offices in

Walworth County by 1840. Captain Israel Williams was appointed as the first post-master in Geneva Bay (later Williams Bay) on May

23, 1844. Geneva Bay Post Office was discontinued in May of 1847 following the death of Israel Williams the previous fall. The post office was re-established with Kiah W. Bailey, postmaster and the post office was moved to his cabin in 1848. The Geneva Bay Post Office was discontinued in 1864, and the

The letter above is historically significant: dated August 1837 it is the first letter received by Captain Williams after his arrival at Geneva Lake in July of that year.[18]

post office at Kiah Bailey's cabin was renamed Bay Hill.

Between 1842 and 1846, the county was rapidly settled. Among the early arrivals were Levi Carey, Stephen Brown, and Bred Brownell in 1843. In 1844, D.P. Handy set up the first blacksmith shop. This was at Delap's Corner, one and one half miles north of Williams Bay. He eventually sold to Anthony Delap. Mr. Bromaghim was another settler in 1844, and in 1845 Jarvis Vincent. Noah John came in the same year. Moses P. Hadley bought the ground where Yerkes Observatory now stands.[19,20]

The twenty years following 1850 were somewhat uneventful in Williams Bay and the surrounding district. The country developed; the forest gave way to broad productive fields. Old settlers died or moved away, and new ones took their places. Boys grew into men and tilled the fields their fathers had rescued from the wilderness. Geneva Lake, nestling among the hills of Walworth County, was becoming known as the most brilliant jewel of all that magnificent collection of lakes and streams in southern Wisconsin and northern Illinois.

At the foot of the lake lay Geneva, a beautiful and thriving village that had developed from the three log cabins of 1837. At its head, Fontana, a cluster of houses surrounded Douglass' Mills, which supplied flour and ground feed to farmers for miles around. At Williams Bay the old Williams farm house still stood alone and no indications of a village were seen. Robert Russell was back again, living on what is now part of Yerkes Observatory. Between him and the Williams farm lived Joseph Stam, a recent settler. On the hillside north of the Bay, Jonas G. Southwick, who had settled there in 1849, raised a family of children, who became respected citizens of the community. Near where the railroad crossed under Route 50 were the log cabins of Lige Godfrey, Jeremiah Ward, and the farm of Festus A. Williams. This area would later become the site of A. H. Harris' Spanish-style home with its red tile roof overlooking Geneva and Como Lakes and Kemah Farm where Mr. Harris bred and raised his legendary prized Arabian horses.

Other early settlers include: the Barnhart Family, Kiah W. Bailey, John Handy, and J.T. Paddock. Near East Delavan were Job Williams, Samuel and Ira Utter, L. H. Willis, H. Beals, Daniel P. Handy, Mrs. Laura Bailey, Mrs. Clarissa Wright, Lucy Pierce, Jerre P. Ward, Mrs. Ward, Nelson Catkins, Elihu Eaton, and Mrs. Clarissa Vincent. The first Doctor at the Bay was Dr. Strang who lived to the west of what became George Williams Golf Course. George Southwick, father of Oliver P. Southwick, also lived near what became the golf course. Across the Bay was Otis Dodge. On the rise of ground above the Lions Field House was the Peter Robertson cabin. The Kiah Bailey family had a cabin on the north side of Geneva Street on the site of the Bailey House across from the drive to Yerkes Observatory. Edward B. Hollister lived toward Elkhorn and was the father of Albert Hollister and grandfather of Edward and Lawrence. It is hard to image that the premium lake front lots that are now part of Conference Point were "woodlots" used by farmers at that time to build barns and outbuildings for their more flat, fertile and farmable land inland from Geneva Lake. W.B. Van Schack from Big Foot Prairie paid $300 for the Point and after using wood off it for several years sold it for $500. At one point Jonas Southwick had been offered the 40 acres on the point for a cow, but refused the offer.

EAST DELAVAN

In the early years residents of the Village of Williams Bay and surrounding area had to travel to neighboring towns for supplies. The road to Geneva/Lake Geneva was practically impassable for part of the year so supplies had to be purchased in East Delavan,

Douglass' Corner (Walworth), Elkhorn, or Delavan. Village residents also had to travel to neighboring towns to attend church services. Until 1891, the closest churches were near the intersection of the current Highway 67 and County road F, East Delavan, and the Latter Day Saints church (now the Belfry Theatre) on Elkhorn Road north of the Village.

East Delavan was a thriving community, complete with church, school, blacksmith, horse doctor, creamery, and store plus a number of houses. Thus East Delavan was a community long before Williams Bay. The school was the East Delavan School, District No. 2, of the town of Delavan. The first log schoolhouse was built in 1845 and was used until it was replaced by a frame building in 1870. The land for the school and church was donated by C. Woodford, who owned a blacksmith shop and farm near East Delavan.

The Baptist Church was organized on February 14, 1845. The Rev. Henry Topping of Delavan was invited to the

Sketch of East Delavan circa 1880s. Photo credit: Walworth County Historical Society.

organizational meeting. The church had 17 charter members who first met in the log school house and erected the first church building in 1846. In 1868 it was decided that the church was too small and run down so a new one was started. A white wood church was completed in 1869 at a cost of $2,327. Dedication was Feb. 16, 1870.[21]

The creamery was on the north side of the road, and burned in June 1911, but was rebuilt and continued operation. It produced about 3,500 pounds of butter each month.[22] The East Delavan Post Office was established in 1872, a station on the Star Route (mail carrier) from Elkhorn to Harvard. At that time it served a community of about a dozen dwellings and about 50 citizens.

East Delavan Union Cemetery was formally established in 1854 but the first burial took place in 1843 on land owned by Samuel

Utter after the accidental death of Alexander Utter, who died when the well he was helping to dig on his uncle's property caved in. Many of the early settlers of Williams Bay are buried in this cemetery including Captain Williams, Lavina Williams, Austin, and Moses Williams, and Mrs. Williams' mother Mrs. Hannah Joy.

After the Chicago & North Western railway was extended to Williams Bay in 1888, some of the residents of East Delavan realized the advantages of rail service and moved to Williams Bay.

CIVIL WAR

On Monday, April 15, 1861 the Governor of Wisconsin, Alexander W. Randall received the following dispatch from the Secretary of War: "To His Excellency A. W. Randall, Governor of Wisconsin: Call made on you by tonight's mail, for one (1) regiment of militia for immediate service, Simon Cameron, Secretary of War." The following day Governor Randall issued the proclamation calling for volunteers. Within seven days, thirty-six companies had volunteered their services; among the first was one from Geneva—the 4th Wisconsin Cavalry Company F. The companies were ordered to Madison and upon arrival the men found that their enlistment was for three years instead of three months. Those who wished could back down but only one man took advantage of it. As the war dragged, many more men were called to serve in the Union Army.

BEGINNING OF THE VILLAGE

In 1870, Festus Williams returned from Virginia, where he had been superintendent of a large plantation near historic Jamestown he took up residence in Beloit; in 1874 he came back to the village to farm the marsh lands extending toward the Bay today known as Kishwaketoe Nature Conservancy.

A man who is worthy of more than a passing notice is Major Edward Brown Meatyard. For nearly twenty years he was one of the most prominent men in the area of Geneva Lake. His house, known as Lawn Glen, was built near the lake shore east of Cedar Point, at a cost of several thousand dollars and showed a decided English style. He invested in land about Williams Bay, owning 240 acres in the town of Walworth and 600 acres of land in the towns of Linn and Geneva that extended from the lake shore east of Cedar Point over the ridge and embracing all the flat land at the head of Lake Como. He invested large amounts of money trying to reclaim this swampland, but his efforts were fruitless. Meatyard was a Geneva Lake enthusiast and made himself thoroughly familiar with the topography of all the surrounding area. He spent a great deal of time and money perfecting various inventions, but realized little gain from them. His fortune dwindled away until nearly everything was lost. His property at Cedar Point was sold for back taxes in 1889 and passed into the hands of John Johnston Jr.

E. L. Baker, a surveyor and civil engineer whose home was in Lake Geneva, had long had a plan which at first thought appears wild and impossible, and as it failed we may say it was a hair-brained scheme. Had it succeeded it would have been a grand triumph of genius.

The plan was as follows: buy up all the land about Lake Como at as low a price as possible, dam up the outlet of Lake Como, and raise that body of water to a level with Lake Geneva (It is about 14 feet lower), dig a channel, large enough for the passage of any boat in Lake Geneva, from Williams Bay to Lake Como. Had this plan been feasible it would have made the shoreline of Como Lake as valuable as the shoreline of Geneva Lake

In the meantime a flourishing settlement was springing up on the west side of the Bay around the old farm house built by Captain Williams. In 1883 James W. Loft bought a five-acre tract of land on the south side of the Williams farm and built a residence. The Williams homestead was now owned and occupied by Lucretia, widow of Royal Williams, and her youngest son Harley.

In 1889 a subdivision, was laid out by Surveyor J. L. Tubbs, of Elkhorn. W. G. DeGroff was the first to purchase a lot (on the corner of Walworth Avenue, Elkhorn Road, and Geneva Street) and built his residence that summer. The next purchasers were Arne H. Arneson and Peter Stenstrom, who bought and built on the hill above the Williams farm house. In the spring of 1889, John Hansen bought five acres from Lucretia Williams and built a house on the south side of the Williams farm.

During the next two years village development was slow. The town line road (Elkhorn Road or Highway 67) was laid out from Jonas Southwick's farm south to the Village, and other minor improvements were made. In 1891 Arne H. Arneson, Eric Anderson, and G. L. Jensen incorporated the Scandinavian Free Lutheran church, bought a lot, and erected a church building.

In February 1892, Marie R. Williams, wife of Edward F. Williams (Royal Williams' second son) secured appointment as postmistress and the Williams Bay post office was established. For the first two years the mail was brought from Lake Geneva by team; at first only bi-weekly, but the business steadily increased, and during 1893 it was brought daily. In the fall of 1894, through the efforts of the postmistress and her husband who was her deputy, the mail route was transferred to the railroad, and in the fall of 1895 the Village began to receive two mail deliveries per day, which continued until the 1960s.

The winter of 1893 Henry McBride and Frank Harville purchased land on the east side of the town line road from Harley Williams for an Ice house. They organized the Lake Geneva Ice Co., and built one of the largest ice houses in Wisconsin. It had a capacity of 40,000 tons, employed 125 men for about six weeks during the winter, and from five to 15 men during the shipping season.

In the spring of 1893, C. M. Williams came from Lyons and purchased the corner across from W. G. DeGroff's and erected the Lake Vista Hotel and opened up a hotel and general store business.

In the same year Harley Williams opened a coal, lime, and brick business. Beginning in a small way he had gradually worked up an extensive and lucrative business.

During the winter of 1892 - 1893, Dr. M. E. LeClerque, of Chicago purchased sixty acres of the flat land north of the depot (now Kishwauketoe), organizing the Williams Bay Land Company. He laid out his purchase into blocks and lots and commenced improvements. Money did not seem to be forthcoming as readily as might have been expected, but nobody felt alarmed, as it was reported that the company was worth millions. It was just before the opening of the Columbian Exposition World's Fair in Chicago and times were good, wages were high, and the country was flourishing. It looked as if the Village on Geneva Lake was going to "boom", and no doubt it would have done so but for the financial crash that struck the country that summer. When the crash came in July, the Williams Bay Land Company was struck a death blow.

In 1895 there was a demand for more lots, and another addition was laid out on the hill above the original subdivision (west of the library on Williams Street). Meanwhile several houses had been built, all of them a credit to the growing village. Among the most important were those were built by Eric Anderson, A. Blix, Harley Williams, Henry Francis, U. Lockwood, W. G. DeGroff, and C. Slocomb.

Christian Hansen subdivided part of his farm east of the Bay and called it Hansen's Addition to Williams Bay in 1894.

In 1894 W. A. Lackey secured complete control of the livery from Williams Bay to Delavan Lake and leased land from the railroad company for a barn. He established a livery business and had a large and well-ordered stable, rigs, and conveyances for his customers.

In January 1895 L. E. Francis commenced the erection of a store building and upon its completion, opened up a stock of groceries and general merchandise. J. Rouse purchased the business and enlarged the building and business.

C. M. Williams also made a change in 1895. His business was becoming too large for one person to conveniently handle so he rented the hotel portion of his building to Joseph Keat from Elkhorn. Mr. Williams built an addition on the west side of the store and in partnership with G. S. Holmes was doing an extensive business. Meanwhile under the management of Mr. Keat the Lake Vista House became a popular place.

As the 19th century was coming to a close the community had three subdivisions, one hotel, two stores, a post-office, blacksmith shop, barber shop, and some thirty buildings which were used for residential purposes.

GENEVA LAKES EMERGES AS AN AREA OF SUMMER RESORT,
SEASONAL HOMES, CAMPS, AND RELIGIOUS RETREATS

As the cities of Racine, Milwaukee and Chicago grew with business and industry, so too did the need for fresh air, leisure, and relaxation. Interest in fishing, swimming, and sailing activities began to take

The camps near Williams Bay were in close proximity to each other. The sign in this photo points the way to the different camps. Photo credit: Holiday Home Camp.

hold and soon Geneva Lake began to populate with seasonal residents, vacationers, and campers. Beginning in the 1870s, each summer Geneva Lake attracted more and more visitors who rented rooms in boarding houses or camped along the shore of the lake.

Lovers of rustic life could vacation in a "modern hotel teeming with life, fashion and beauty" or, enjoy nature among parks and wooded camp grounds. The earliest resorts established on Geneva Lake were Kayes Park in 1871 on the south shore. Russell's Forest Glen Park in 1872 on the western end of the lake (later the grounds of the Gardens subdivision and Belvidere Park Association), Montague & Porter's Park in 1873 (later the grounds of Buena Vista Park), and Pishcotaqua Park House in 1880 (later grounds of Knollwood Subdivision) on the north shore. The hotels and cottages could be reached by steamer and were set among beautiful wooded acreage, perfect for camping and relaxation along the tranquil Geneva Lake shoreline. A variety of amenities were offered to guests: bowling alleys, croquet, billiards, play grounds, shooting galleries, row boats, sailing. Kayes Park even had a half-mile race coarse and the Wyant's Museum which contained a collection of taxidermy animals and relics from the aborigines and the south sea islands. These early parks, camps, resorts, and hotels were the precursor to the many others that were to be established in the following decades. Geneva Lake as a resort and camp ground had taken root and would flourish.

Directly across the lake from Kayes Park on a bluff overlooking Williams Bay was Camp Collie. In 1873, Rev. Joseph Collie of the Congregational Church in Delavan established the camp grounds for its members based on the principles: "That the simplest pleasures are the best, and that neither pleasure seeking nor dissipation are recreation. That there are places of recreation needed, not only to retreat from business, but also from the formalities of society." Word of Camp Collie's popularity spread and the camp was open to others. Camp Collie in particular represented a growing social movement that combined religious retreat with the rigors of camping and outdoor recreational activities. Sport and physical activity were thought to build a good moral foundation and character,[23] a framework for the Young Men's Christian Association, Camp Collie, Eleanor Camp, and Olivet Camp.

The Great Chicago Fire occurred in October of 1871 and accelerated the popularity of Geneva Lake as a summer resort area. The fire burned for three days, destroying 3.3 square miles of the city, killing up to 300 people, and leaving more than 100,000 homeless. After the fire, numerous Chicago industrialists sought refuge upon the shore of Geneva Lake while the city was rebuilt. The Chicago & North Western's arrival in Lake Geneva in 1871 made the beautiful location easily accessible and the emergence of large estates on Geneva Lake began. In 1871, Shelton Sturges of Maple Lawn estate was one of the first to build. His architect was famous Henry Lord Gay, who subsequently purchased ground and built a cottage for himself. Then followed Julian Rumsey, Mayor of Chicago who built Shadow Hill in 1873 and George L. Dunlap who built the Moorings in 1874. Dunlap was instrumental in having the Chicago & North Western railroad extended from Crystal Lake to Lake Geneva. It's accessibility made it a natural place for city dwellers to escape the heat and smog of the city.[24]

In William Bay some of the first to arrive and build grand estates on the lakeshore were Edward B. Meatyard, Lawn Glen (1874); Herbert A. Beidler, Alpine Villa (1890); and John M. Smyth, Tyrawley (1895). On the western shores of Williams Bay: Williams S. Harbert, Tre-brah, (Harbert spelled backward-1884); W.J. Chalmers, Dronley (1888); and Patrick J. Healy (1890).[25]

Near the point on the western shore of Williams Bay
Photo credit: Deborah Dumelle Kristmann Collection.

CHICAGO & NORTH WESTERN RAILWAY SERVICE

The first train to Lake Geneva arrived in 1856, but rail service to the area was short lived, for only a few years later service was discontinued due to deterioration of the track. Rail service would not come to Lake Geneva again until the summer of 1871. By the mid 1880s a proposal was made to extend the Chicago & North Western rail line to Williams Bay and then to Delavan and Milton Junction. However, in 1886 it was determined that the line would extend from Lake Geneva to Williams Bay for the summer resort trade and winter ice cutting business after the city of Lake Geneva refused to grant the railroad the right of way to the lake shore. The company received 17 acres of land from Major Meatyard. Fetus A. Williams gave six acres comprising of 1,320 feet of lake shore extending east from where the depot stood. Mrs. Lucretia Williams, widow of Royal Williams, gave 12 acres including the shore line west from the depot to the creek. Ten acres more north of the track were purchased from Mr. Lee and Mr. Nohelty. This gave the railroad company a tract of 45 acres of land, and a lake frontage of about 1,980 feet.

Articles of association were filed with the Wisconsin Secretary of State on August 5, 1887, opening the six mile stretch from Lake Geneva to Williams Bay to extension; grading was begun in the fall of 1887; the track ran a short distance north from the depot in Lake Geneva and turned west to follow the south shore of Duck Lake (Como). After crossing the Delavan Road (highway 50) the track made a "sharp S curve" south and then west along the lakefront in Williams Bay. The new rail line opened on June 1, 1888 with one train making the run to Williams Bay.

Chicago & North Western train near the railroad water tower. Photo credit: Deborah Dumelle Kristmann Collection

An exclusive rail service called the Millionaire's Special carried wealthy Chicagoans to Lake Geneva and Williams Bay on Friday afternoons in the summer. As train time approached private steam yachts lined up along the piers at the lakefront in Williams Bay waiting for their owners to arrive.

In 1965 the decision was made to end rail service to the Village. The last train to Williams Bay arrived at the station on December 31, 1965. Train service to Williams Bay ended when the train left the station for Lake Geneva to await the trip to Chicago on the morning of January 2, 1966.

YERKES OBSERVATORY

In 1890, a unique opportunity was being formulated in the world of astronomy that would soon fall upon the shores of Geneva lake and the growing community in Williams Bay. The University of Southern California planned to build the world's largest refracting telescope, using glass disks cast by Mantois of Paris and polished into 40-inch lenses by Alvan Clark and Sons, Cambridgeport, Massachusetts. When George Ellery Hale learned the University of Southern California abandoned the project for lack of funding, he urged the University of Chicago to acquire the lenses and construct the telescope and an observatory to house it. Hale and William Rainey Harper, president of the University of Chicago, approached transit tycoon Charles Tyson Yerkes, who agreed to fund the facility.

Yerkes 40-inch refracting telescope at the Columbian Exposition. Photo credit: Chicago Tribune.

While Hale and Yerkes were busy making arrangements to build the Observatory, the great telescope itself was put on display at the 1893 World Columbian Exposition in Chicago. The World's Columbian Exposition was organized to commemorate the 400th anniversary of Christopher Columbus's arrival in the new world. The telescope appeared at the north end of the main aisle in Manufacturing Hall. Improvement in telescopes at the time was thought to have reached its limitations with the 36-inch refracting instrument at the Lick Observatory. The new 40-inch refracting lens of the Yerkes telescope would allow scientists to see further into the vastness of space, a monumental breakthrough of its time.

Hale sought to find a perfect location for the observatory: the location had to be close to the University, but beyond the smoke, haze, and city lights of Chicago. On December 9th, 1893 Sherburne

W. Burnham wrote to Hale, informing him that the Williams Bay site had been chosen. The existing railroad line connecting it to Chicago and the 53 acre tract of land off the shores of Geneva made an ideal location for the observatory. Mr. Johnston then donated the land and construction commenced in April of 1895.

There was a new rhythm to the gravel roads of Williams Bay, as many skilled artisans and workers came to the Village to help build the Observatory. Men boarded in local homes and rooming houses; some brought their families and purchased homes. There was a constant flow of people walking to and from the construction site. Meanwhile, the train brought materials which had to be hauled by teams of horses up the road. To be sure, there was a flurry of activity in the village that had never been seen before.

Yerkes Observatory played a pivotal point in the development of Williams Bay. There was much speculation about the many opportunities it would bring to the community that went beyond the construction of the Observatory. Yerkes' great telescope was cutting-edge technology in the field of astronomy; there was great anticipation that the community would grow as scientists, professors, and students affiliated with the prestigious University of Chicago would flock to Williams Bay.

The first astronomical observations with the completed telescope were made by George Ellery Hale and his associates in the summer of 1897. The excellent optical qualities of the new telescope were immediately proven when astronomer

Some of the worlds most renowned astronomers have viewed the heavens at Yerkes Observatory. Photo credit: Yerkes Observatory.

Edward Emerson Barnard discovered a faint third companion to the star Vega, which had gone undetected even by the skilled astronomer Sherburne W. Burnham using the 36-inch Lick telescope.

Attention turned to Williams Bay on October 21, 1897 when a crowd gathered for the official dedication ceremony of the University of Chicago's great Yerkes Observatory. It was a day of speeches, glorifying both the telescope in its Beaux Arts Observatory and the man who made the whole thing possible, Charles Tyson Yerkes.

PROGRESSIVES, SUFFRAGISTS, AND RELIGIOUS FREE THINKERS LIVING IN THE BAY

ORIGINS OF PROGRESSIVISM

- As America entered into the 20th century, middle class reformers addressed many social problems.
- Issues addressed:
  - Working conditions
  - rights for women and children
  - economic reform,
  - environmental issues
  - social welfare

At the turn of the century political, social, and religious movements began to take hold, especially among affluent socialites from large industrialized cities like Chicago. There were three interesting individuals living in Williams Bay who stood out during this time: Dr. Alice Bunker Stockham (b. 1833 - d. 1912), George Chainey (b. 1851- d. 1935), and Elizabeth Boynton Harbert (b. 1843 - d. 1925). They all hailed from Evanston, Illinois, a northern suburb of Chicago on Lake Michigan. And for a time in the early 20th century, they all resided along the western shore of Williams Bay where they actively engaged in their progressive pursuits.

Dr. Alice Bunker Stockham was a widely know obstetrician and gynecologist. She was the fifth woman in the U.S. to become a doctor. She was also an author, publisher, orator, and suffragist. She promoted gender equality, dress reform, birth control, women's health issues, and sexual fulfillment for successful marriages. In 1897 she launched a New Thought School in Williams Bay, called the Vrailia Heights Metaphysical School to provide a site for formal discussions inspired by the 1893 Columbian Exposition and World Congress of Religions. Classes in philosophy, metaphysics, home science, art, and literature were offered in addition to swimming, dance, tennis, and theater. In 1905, when Stockham was in her seventies, the Society for the Suppression of Vice accused her, under the Comstock Law, of sending improper matter through the mails. She hired famed attorney Clarence Darrow and the case went to trial, but she was found guilty and her books banned, forcing her publishing company and school to close.[26]

In 1902, an Italian Renaissance mansion was under construction on the western shore of Williams Bay for a former Methodist Reverend turned "Free Thinking" spiritualist by the name of George Chainey. Free Thought was a philosophical ideology based on science and reason and not restricted by authority, tradition, or religion. Chainey

MAHANAIM SCHOOL OF INTERPRETATION

GEORGE CHAINEY

Author of The Unsealed Bible

FOUNDER AND INSTRUCTOR

The purpose of Mahanaim is to demonstrate, both by teaching and living, the nature of heaven as Revelation, and the perfect knowableness of God, both spiritually and naturally. The means to this end are the study and interpretation of the Sacred Inspired Books of the World, and the comprehension and practice of life from The Universal Standpoint.

CORRESPONDING STUDENTS.

These are furnished with type-written Lessons, supplemented by personal correspondence with the Instructor.

HOME STUDENTS.

These enjoy the benefit of daily instruction and practice with the Instructor.

became a nationally known and authoritative figure in the area of "free thought and spiritualism." Before his move to Williams Bay, Chainey had used the Fine Arts Building on Michigan Avenue as headquarters for his "School of Interpretation". It is there that he wrote and orated on the subject of his life's work, the *Unsealed Bible*. The school was short-lived in Williams Bay, Chainey moved to Long Beach, California, where he continued his spiritual endeavors. The estate changed hands and became known as the Ferndale Inn until the mid 1940s.

Elizabeth Boynton Harbert who attended Western Female Seminary in Ohio and Terre Haute Female College, was an author, suffrage movement leader, and the first woman to design and secure a woman's rights platform in a major political party. Many influential guests stayed at the Harbert summer home Tre-brah, including Susan B. Anthony. The Harberts hosted many informative educational, social, and political lectures given by orators with like-minded viewpoints such as Alice B. Stockham and George Chainey.

THE VILLAGE OF WILLIAMS BAY

The Village of Williams Bay had grown to an estimated 300 by 1896. A permanent post office under the name of Williams Bay was established in 1892. The Lake Vista Hotel was built on the present-day Lackey block in 1893. The year 1893 proved to be a year of great building activity. In April of that year, the Williams farm had been platted into three subdivisions and by November fifteen houses were under construction, adding to the eight houses that had been completed earlier in the year.

In 1918, an association of seventeen citizens was formed to sponsor the purchase of high quality motion picture equipment. A

The Village of Williams Bay as it looked in 1897. Photo credit: Terry Thomas Collection.

nominal charge was paid by community members to view high quality motion pictures. Profits were used to outfit the needs of the new public library and after the equipment had paid for itself and provided years of income to the new public library, the equipment was turned over to the school.[27]

The village was incorporated after a group of residents consisting of Dr. E.J. Fucik, William Valentine, S.J. Noble, Gottllieb Henne, Andrew Carlquist, Alfred Pihl, Lawrence A. Hollister, Walter E. Jewell, Andrew Anderson, Oscar M. Waterbury, and A.B. Carlson signed a petition asking that the Village of Williams Bay be incorporated in June 1919.

On June 26, 1919 a survey was circulated to residents of the Village and $81 was collected to pay incorporation expenses. Lawrence Hollister conducted a census finding that as of August 2, 1919 there were 492 people living in the area of the Village which was to be incorporated.

William Child was the surveyor who laid out the village. The area to be incorporated contained 1,114 acres of land; bounded on the south by 19,520 feet of lake shore, on the west by Delavan Road, on the north by the township lines of Delavan and Geneva, and on the east by the Peter Johnson farm.

Incorporation was granted by Circuit Court Judge Grimm on September 15, 1919 and the incorporation papers were recorded on October 23, 1919.

On October 23, 1919 the men living in the Village voted whether or not to incorporate. Those serving as members of the Election Board were E.H. Hollister, Clerk; Henry Granzow and Arne H. Arneson, Ballot Clerks; Harry Brumgard and S.B. Barrett, Inspectors. Total voters registered: 108; Voted for: 66; Voted against: 41; Void vote: 1.

The first meeting of the new Village Board was held on November 24, 1919. The first elected Village officials were:

President: Storrs B. Barrett
Clerk: Oliver J. Lee
Treasurer: Arthur Anderson
Assessor: Arne H. Arneson
Constable: Carl M. Bjorge
Supervisor: J.A. Parkhurst
Justice of the Peace: L.A. Hollister
Trustees: Henry W. Granzow, Harry V. Brumgard, Edwin B. Frost, John Andell, John Lackey, and Alfred Pihl

In 1922 the Village contracted Jacob L. Crane to create a Development plan for the newly formed Village of Williams Bay. The Crane Development Plan proposed moving the railroad station back to allow a lake front park and promenade, a "public square" between Walworth Avenue and Elkhorn Road, a combination water tower and look-out tower, decorative street lights, and more.

Accomplishments in the twenty years following incorporation

included street lights, the purchase of a fire engine and equipment, Frost Park, improved streets, paved Geneva Street, garage for Village trucks and equipment, water plant with purification and softening system, sewage disposal plant, purchase of lake

Circa 1930s Edgewater Park. Photo credit: Barrett Memorial Library.

shore from the railroad with the beginning of improvements, provided aid to school for an addition, extended water mains, purchased land for Edgewater Park for $10,000, and bathing pier with life guards.[28]

CONTINUED GROWTH THROUGH DIFFICULT TIMES

As the nation was drawn into wars, the ratification of the 18th Amendment to the Constitution which banned the manufacture, transportation, and sale of intoxicating liquors (Prohibition), and economic depressions, no one was spared the grim consequences. Like others across the nation residents of Williams Bay lost loved ones, jobs, money, property, and businesses. Despite these difficulties, the village would continue to grow and its residents thrived.[29]

The land bounded by Collie, Geneva and Congress Streets, which was owned by Rev. Carl A. Tolin and others, was platted and recorded on August 11, 1920. It included the lake shore from the lines between Holiday Home and Olivet Camp (Norman B. Barr Camp), Delavan Road (Theatre Road) to a line between Walworth and Delavan, Linn, and Geneva Townships.

The real development of the Bay seems to date from Arthur B. Jensen and Donald F. Abel, platting Lock Vista Club no. 1, recorded October 31, 1921. Mr. Jensen's sales ability which has been demonstrate several times since in subdivisions called attention to Williams Bay as a superb resort for people of modest incomes. It went so well that Lock Vista Club no. 2 was platted and recorded August 11, 1922.

Will Lackey and his brother Reuben platted Oakwood Estates and recorded it as Lackey Bros. Subdivision July 20, 1923 which had become largely an all year round home community.

Walter Jewell platted part of his property as Jewell's Subdivision and recorded it September 23, 1924.

Summer Haven was put on sale after the land was purchased from George Williams Estate by Wisconsin Transportation Co. which had used it for storage of its boats for many years.

Then Emory F. Jaeger and Alfred A. Pederson who were partners in an awning business in Chicago and spent many summers in the Bay, conceived the idea of platting the H. A. Beidler farm with its lake shore home grounds and calling the development Cedar Point Park. The lots sold so fast that the plat recorded May 19, 1923 was nearly sold out. With such success Jaeger and Pederson were encouraged to buy from the N. K. Fairbank Estate all the land along the Bay and lay it out into what is said to be the most beautiful subdivision on Geneva Lake. The plats called for Cedar Point Park, Additions No. 1, 2, and 3. In all there were platted 470 lots.

The fine advertising of Jaeger & Pederson to Chicagoans brought Williams Bay to the front as a plan for one's summer home. With the prosperity of the middle twenties, Chicago and Suburban Chicago area residents had money for summer and winter homes and came in large numbers to look over the properties, by auto and special trains. The restrictions kept the sales to a very limited group of people. As of 1940, there were 140 homes, many used year round.

By 1930, the permanent population of Williams Bay was 630. This number represented an increase of 44% from 1920, making Williams Bay the fastest growing village in Walworth County. During the busy summer when seasonal residents, hotels, resorts and camps are at their peak, the population in the village would range from 2,000 to over 3,000 at its peak.[30]

CONCLUSION

In closing, we believe this introduction to the history of Williams Bay will be interesting to the majority of our readers. We bring our account of the history to a close for the present and leave the rest for the hand of time and others to write.

Whether a life-long resident or a first time visitor the lyrics to *Moonlight Melody of Williams Bay*[31] the official song of the Village, are sure to ring true "...Maybe the love song moon beams play will bring you back to Williams Bay always a cherished memory..."

Footnotes:

[1] To accompany Northern Boundry of Ohio, and Admission of Michigan into the Union, March 2, 1836

[2] *History and Indian Remains - Lake Geneva and Lake Como*, Paul B. Jenkins and Charles E. Brown

[3] The Wisconsin Archaeologist, Vol. 11, No. 2, The Geneva Lake Centennial, Paul B. Jenkins

[4] *Wau-bun*, Juliette Kinzie (1856)

[5] Bay Leaves, Van Epps

[6] *The History of Wisconsin vols. 2 and 3* (Madison: State Historical Society of Wisconsin)

[7] *Wisconsin: A History,* Robert C. Nesbit (Madison: University of Wisconsin Press, 1973)

[8] *Ethnic Groups in Wisconsin: Historical Background*, Max Kade Institute for German-American Studies (online at http://mki.wisc.edu/)]

[9] Certificates issued by the Governor of Massachusetts declaring Israel Williams elected military posts are located at the Barrett Memorial Library, these documents repudiate previously recorded historical accounts

[10] Ashfield Historical Society, Nancy Garvin

[11] *History and Indian Remains - Lake Geneva and Lake Como*, Paul B. Jenkins and Charles

E. Brown

[12] Bay Leaves Volume 3, No. 1 May 16, 1935 Source: Paul B Jenkins and Charles E. Brown, History and Indian Remains of Lake Geneva and Lake Como Walworth County, Wisconsin

[13] *History of Walworth County*, 1882

[14] Letter from Israel Williams Jr.

[15] Williams Bay Observer 1896-1897

[16] *History and Indian Remains - Lake Geneva and Lake Como*, Paul B. Jenkins and Charles E. Brown

[17] Letters to his family dating from the gold fields of California to his wife and children in Spring Prairie, Walworth County, Wisconsin and one letter written to his brother in Unadilla, Otsego County., New York from September 25, 1852 - August 26, 1855 are in the University of Berkeley Library archives

[18] Letter dated August 1837 to Captain Israel Williams from his son Francis who remained in Massachusetts when the family left for Wisconsin in July of 1837, source: David Valley Collection

[19] Source: Williams Bay Observer 1896-1897

[20] *History and Indian Remains - Lake Geneva and Lake Como*, Paul B. Jenkins and Charles E. Brown

[21] East Delavan Baptist Church

[22] *History of Walworth County*, Clayton Beckwith 1912

[23] *History of Walworth County, Wisconsin*, Brookhaven Press

[24] *Chicago Tribune, June 6, 1898*

[25] *Lake Geneva Newport of the West 1870-1920*, Ann Wolfmeyer and Mary Burns Gage

[26] The Chicago Daily Tribune, Tuesday June 6, 1905

[27] Storrs B. Barrett, 6/18/31

[28] Bay Leaves, Van Epps

[29] Bay Leaves: Volume 7, No. 13 March 30, 1939

[30] Bay Leaves: Vol. 7, No. 13 March 30, 1939

[31] *Moonlight Melody of Williams Bay*, composed by Stanford R. Espedal

May 20, 2017 Looking east Williams Bay lakefront. Photo credit: Grandpa's Big Book - Carol Stenstrom Ortiz.

Chapter 1

THE HEART OF THE VILLAGE
LOCAL BUSINESSES/PROPRIETORS/FIRE DEPARTMENT

Prior to the arrival of the Chicago & North Western Railroad in 1888, Williams Bay was a small rural community. Everything changed when access by train made the village and Geneva Lake more accessible to businesses, home owners, visitors and campers. It was that ease of access that also contributed to Williams Bay being the choice location for the prestigious Yerkes Observatory in 1893. Speculation for an influx of professors and students to the growing community fueled the development of many subdivisions. By the beginning of the twentieth century the little village on Geneva Lake had a library, post office, stores, hotels, and camps.

Circa 1897 The village of Williams Bay and Yerkes Observatory from east of town. The train tracks run parallel to the fence line. The fields were owned by Lucretia Williams and Festus Williams and are now the location of Kishwauketoe Nature Conservancy. Photo Credit: University of Chicago Photographic Archive, apf6-00826, Special Collections Research Center, University of Chicago Library.

Circa 1895 The Lake Vista House was located on the corner of what is now Geneva Street and Walworth Avenue. Joe Keat rented the hotel part of C.M. Williams store and called it Lake Vista House Hotel. Besides the hotel, the building had a pool hall, tavern, meat market, and general merchandise store. The Lake Vista Hotel caught fire and burned down on a cold winter night in 1903. Photo credit: James Wallace Photo Collection, courtesy of Kate Morris Dickerson and Family.

The Lake Vista House Hotel was a large three-story framed structure. It was the second hotel built in Williams Bay, the first was the Buckhorn Tavern, a stop on the stage coach route to Beloit, owned by Captain Israel Williams.

The hotel burned to the ground in 1903. William A. Lackey rebuilt on the site and called the new three-story brick structure the Lackey Building.

Lake Vista Hotel.

A. J. GOODRICH,

PROPRIETOR.

LIVERY

IN CONNECTION.

WILLIAMS BAY, WIS.

LAKE VISTA HOUSE, WILLIAMS BAY, WIS.—
Good boating and fishing; board from $5 to $6
per week; one block from steamer docks.
A. J. GOODRICH,
Lock Box 3.
Williams Bay, Wis.

Circa 1901-1902 Advertisements for the Lake Vista Hotel and Livery owned by A. J. Goodrich. Photo credit: Barrett Memorial Library and Chicago Daily Tribune.

Circa 1897 View of Williams Bay from the east. In the center of the picture is the Lake Vista Hotel and A.J. Goodrich's Livery is in the foreground. To the left of the livery is W.A. Lackey's lumber yard and to the right is the Knickerbocker Ice House. Heading west out of town past the Lake Vista Hotel on the upper right of the photo is the Williams family homestead. Photo credit: Terry Thomas Collection.

Circa 1910 View of Williams Bay from the area of Southwick Creek. The house on the left foreground was the Edward Williams home located in the area of Edgewater Park. The home was the location of the first library and US Post Office. When Marie Williams was named Postmistress in 1892, the name "Williams Bay" was first used for the Village. Mail was first brought by horse and wagon twice a week; later mail was delivered to the Village by rail. In 1895, there were two mail deliveries daily. The large home behind the Williams home was the Ferndale Inn. The large building in the center was a livery barn owned by a man named Schroeder, and the small building to the left was Tully's Meat Market and Hansen's Garage. Photo credit: Deborah Dumelle Kristmann Collection.

Circa 1905 Southwick's General Merchandise was located at the current location of the BayView Building. Oliver Perry and Mary Arline (Ladd) Southwick built this building after their grocery store was destroyed when the adjoining Lake Vista Hotel caught fire. Photo credit: Deborah Dumelle Kristmann Collection.

Circa 1905 Oliver and Mary Southwick had one daughter Arline (born in 1904) who helped in the store as a young girl. Mary died from cancer in 1927. Oliver Southwick died in 1934. Arline attended Whitewater Normal and taught at Sheboygan for four years, returning to Williams Bay to marry Harold Pierce. She was the librarian at Barrett Memorial Library for twelve years. Arline died in 1987. Photo credit: Deborah Dumelle Kristmann Collection.

Circa 1905 Granzow and Peterson, dealers in general merchandise—chiefly staples and fancy groceries, etc. The Granzow and Peterson partnership was formed in 1904. At that time they were in a one-room store, but their trade was constantly growing and about 1908 expanded to the adjoining store with two large business rooms, well arranged and neatly kept. They carried a large and carefully selected stock of up-to-date goods. Their high class and extensive trade brought in customers from remote sections of this part of the county. A fire in 1912 destroyed this building and the grocery store was moved to the Lackey Building. Photo credit: Terry Thomas Collection.

1914 Michael Tobias Peterson in the Granzow and Peterson delivery wagon. Michael Peterson was 19 years of age when he went into partnership with Henry Granzow. Victor Hansen's garage and Tully's Meat Market are in the background. This is now the location of the Williams Bay Fire Dept. Photo credit: The United Church of Christ (Congregational) - Williams Bay.

Circa 1906 The Lackey Building was built in 1905 by W.A. Lackey where the Lake Vista Hotel stood. Mr. Lackey operated a hardware store and a dry goods store next to the post office on the south side of the building. Photo credit: Deborah Dumelle Kristmann Collection.

Circa 1907 Miss Anna Peterson was appointed postmistress in October, 1907. Prior to her appointment to the position she had been a clerk in the local post office for six years. At the time she was one of the youngest postmasters in the state of Wisconsin. Photo credit: The United Church of Christ (Congregational) - Williams Bay.

1913 Anna Radley, Star Route Rural Carrier, between Fontana and Williams Bay delivering mail to Yerkes Observatory. When Star Route contracts were originally awarded, contractors had to be at least 16 years old; in 1902 the age limit for carriers was raised to 21. Contractors were bonded and took an oath of office. Star Route mail carriers traveled by horse or horse-drawn vehicle until the early 1900s. Photo credit: University of Chicago Photographic Archive, apf6-04457, Special Collections Research Center, University of Chicago Library.

1914 Mail time! The first post office for the area was listed as "Geneva Bay" (now known as the Village of Williams Bay) in 1844 and operated in Israel Williams' home. The first post office known as Williams Bay was established in 1892 and was in the home of Edward and Marie Williams. Mail was brought from Lake Geneva three times a week at first, then daily during the summer of 1893. When Mr. and Mrs. Edward Williams retired from their postmaster position in 1898, the office was moved to the DeGroff building on the northeast corner of Walworth Avenue and Geneva Street. Mrs. Josephine Barnhardt became postmistress and Miss Ethel Hatch was a clerk. In 1906, the post office moved directly across Walworth Avenue to the newly constructed Lackey building. Photo credit: The United Church of Christ (Congregational) - Williams Bay.

Circa 1910 A pool hall operated by Roy Colby was located on the lower level of the southeast corner of the Lackey Building; Granzow and Peterson grocery store was next to the pool hall; a tea room which later became R. M. Calkins & Son Restaurant and Bakery was next to the grocery store. Williams Bay Hand Laundry was located in the building that stood just north of the Lackey Building on Walworth Avenue. Photo credit: Deborah Dumelle Kristmann Collection.

Circa 1910 There were at one point two hand laundries in town: Williams Bay Hand Laundry, Edwin Holm, proprietor and Domestic Hand Laundry, Annie Andrews, proprietor. Photo credit: Grandpa's Big Book-Carol Stenstrom Ortiz.

1914 R. M. Calkins & Son Restaurant and Bakery on Walworth Avenue. Village residents were able to get Schmidt Bros. Ice Cream at the restaurant and bakery. Schmidt Bros. Ice Cream was made in Elkhorn. Later generations were able to get ice cream and ice cream sodas at Amundsen's which was also located here. Photo credit: The United Church of Christ (Congregational) - Williams Bay.

Circa 1915 Intersection of Geneva Street and Walworth Avenue. Photo credit: Deborah Dumelle Kristmann Collection.

Circa 1920s Sawyer's Grocery and Butcher Shop was located at the southeast corner of Geneva Street. and Walworth Avenue. This location also housed Carlson Grocery and later the Fish Line Grocery Store. Photo credit: David Valley.

Circa 1920s Southeast corner of Geneva Street and Walworth Avenue: Sawyer's Grocery Store Groceries and Meat Cash & Carry. Hopkins and Walker Garage was on the corner across from the grocery store. Notice the street light in the upper right corner of the photo. Southwick's Mercantile can be seen in the center of the background. Early Williams Bay physician Dr. Edward Fucik's office was between the Lackey Building and Southwick's store. Photo credit: Williams Bay Historical Society.

A. HOLLISTER & SONS LUMBER YARD

Albert Hollister was the son of a pioneer, born on his parent's farm between Williams Bay and Elkhorn in 1854. Albert attended school in Elkhorn. After getting his education he taught school about 4 miles north of Elkhorn for four years. Albert then went to Juneau County where he taught school for four more years.

His interest in lumber began during a year spent in Denver where he worked in a lumber yard. His first venture in the lumber business was in Ionia, Iowa. In 1910, Albert had a chance to sell his lumber yards in Iowa and Illinois. Albert kept the lumber yard in Belvidere, Illinois and moved back to Delavan.

In 1911 the lumber yard in Williams Bay was purchased from W. A. Lackey. Albert's sons Edward and Lawrence came to Williams Bay to live and work for their father at A. Hollister and Sons Lumber Company.

Photo credits: Grass Roots Lake Geneva; Williams Bay Historical Society; and Deborah Dumelle Kristmann Collection.

1914 A blacksmith shop stood just north of the present post office. It was owned by Oscar Roeker and later Louis Rasmussen. Photo credit: The United Church of Christ (Congregational) - Williams Bay.

Circa 1910 Charles Southwick lived in the house located at 38 W Geneva. The Southwick's operated a boarding house called the Bayview Inn at the location for several years. Charles Southwick was an uncle of Oliver Southwick who owned and operated Southwick's General Merchandise store. The Bayview Inn was located next door to Oliver Southwick's store. Photo Credit: Barrett Memorial Library.

46

Circa 1908 The first library was located in the home of Edward and Marie Williams. The Williams home was located near the Bay in what is now Edgewater Park. Books were supplied by the Wisconsin Free Library Commission. In 1901, Storrs B. Barrett was instrumental in bringing a traveling library wagon to Williams Bay. Mr. Barrett led the drive to add a designated library building to the community. Lake Geneva resident George Sturges offered to donate a 48 x 29 foot clubhouse from his lakefront home along with a $1,000 donation. Legend differs on how the building was moved. One version says it was brought over the frozen lake; another that it was brought by land when the ice broke up early; and one that claims part of the building was brought over the ice and the rest was moved by land after an early thaw. In 1919, when the Village of Williams Bay was incorporated, the Library Association was able to turn the library and its contents over to the village free of debt. In 1939, two years after the death of Storrs Barrett, the village board voted to commemorate the man whose efforts brought books and a library to its residents, renaming the Williams Bay Library the Storrs Barrett Memorial Library. Photo credit: Barrett Memorial Library.

Circa 1908 George Williams, grandson of Israel Williams, outside Barrett Memorial Library. George acted as caretaker tending to the fire to keep the library warm in the winter. George never married and lived in the family homestead until his death in 1924. Photo Credit: Barrett Memorial Library.

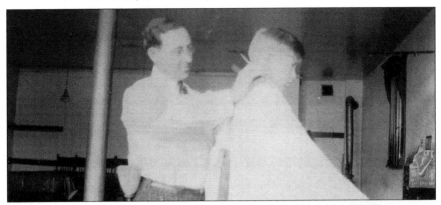

1914 George L. Goodrich was the proprietor of the barber shop in the early 1900s. His barber shop was in the Lackey Building on Walworth Avenue. Mr. Goodrich was also an agent for the Delavan Steam Laundry. In 1933 Mr. Goodrich returned to Williams Bay to assist William Elbert in his barber shop for the summer. Photo credit: The United Church of Christ (Congregational) - Williams Bay.

CEO. L. COODRICH,
Barber and Hairdresser.
☞ Keen razors, sharp shears and good work guaranteed.
☞ Agent for Delavan Steam Laundry.
WILLIAMS BAY, WISCONSIN.

Williams Bay
BARBER SHOP

Wm. L. Elbert, Prop.

Hair Cuts   35¢
Shower Baths   25¢

PANTORIUM AGENCY
Dry Cleaning

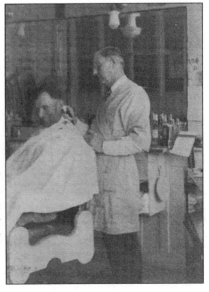

Circa Unknown William Elbert opened his barber shop in the Lackey Building on Walworth Avenue in the 1920s. Mr. Elbert was an agent for Pantorium Dry Cleaning. Terry Thomas purchased the barber shop when Mr. Elbert retired. Photo credit: Terry Thomas Collection.

Circa 1919 Hansen's Auto Repair, owned by Victor Hansen, was located near the present Fire Department at the intersection of Geneva Street and Highway 67. Young Victor Hansen is standing under the sign. Photo Credit: Tom and Kathy Leith.

Circa 1920s Cadillac used by Hansen Livery Service to take travelers from the train depot in Williams Bay to Lake Lawn Lodge in nearby Delavan. Photo Credit: Tom and Kathy Leith.

Circa 1925 Hopkins and Walker Garage on the southwest corner of Geneva Street and Walworth Avenue. Elmer H. Hopkins and Frank W. Walker formed a partnership in 1923 to buy out the business of George Van Velzer. At that time there was only a small brick garage on the corner. (Having been an aircraft mechanic for the US Army in France during the First World War, Elmer, a.k.a Hoppi, could fix anything with a motor.) Before coming to Williams Bay he worked in Hebron and Sharon. Frank Walker had the business experience. Pictured Left to Right: John Powers, Bert Willis, Ole Peterson, and Victor Hansen. Photo credit: Carl Hanley.

Circa 1925 As Williams Bay grew it became necessary to expand by rebuilding and enlarging the garage. A lot was purchased next to the garage and the boat storage area was added. After Hopkins and Walker sold the garage in the 1930s, Hopkins opened a marina and worked there until he closed the business in the early 1950's. Photo credit: Carl Hanley.

Circa 1930s After closing Hopkins and Walker Garage, Elmer "Hoppi" Hopkins opened Hopkins Marine Service. The marine service was a factory authorized service location for Johnson Outboard Motors. After closing the marine service, "Hoppi" sold the Johnson franchise to Gage Marine in exchange for a job for life. Hopkins died in 1971 at age 84. Photo credit: Carl Hanley.

Circa 1930s Bay Oil Company was founded and owned by Frank Arthur Anderson. F. A. Anderson sold Bay Oil Company to Lee L. Clayton in June of 1935. The garage was originally located on the corner of Walworth Avenue and Geneva Street, the former location of Hopkins and Walker Garage. F. A. Anderson was the son of Eric Anderson, proprietor of the Fernwood Inn and Twin Cottage Resort. Later the corner would become a Mobil gas station and garage, Mitchell and Maxon proprietors. The Williams homestead is visible in the background. Photo credit: Catsy and Julie Johnson.

The early Bay Oil Company truck parked on Walworth Avenue Normandie Hotel is in the background. Photo credit: John A. Anderson.

```
     BAY OIL COMPANY

      Service Station
       ON THE CORNER

  Complete Garage Service
```

Circa 1930s Bay Oil moved across from Edgewater Park on Geneva Street (current sail rigging area by Cafe Calamari). Photo credit: John A. Anderson.

Circa 1936 Visitors to Williams Bay could rent a bicycle from Bud Johnson for 25¢ per hour to take a ride around town. Photo credit: Michelle Bie Love.

Circa 1920s Bicycles had become an important form of transportation and recreation in the early 1900s. Kids rode their bikes everywhere: school, grocery store, post office, and beach. Photo credit: Grandpa's Big Book - Carol Stenstrom Ortiz.

VOLUNTEER FIRE DEPARTMENT

Over 90 years ago the Williams Bay Volunteer Fire Department was organized with 15 members. Victor Hansen, charter member and first Fire Chief, served in that position for 33 years. The Fire Committee at the time was: Dr. E.J. Fucik, W.A. Lackey, and E.H. Hollister. The newly organized department's first Stoughton fire engine was purchased for $5,130, a considerable sum in 1923.

The department used rented quarters for meetings and equipment storage until 1936 when

Circa 1923 The newly organized department's first Stoughton fire engine. Photo credit: Tom and Kathy Leith.

members built their new firehouse at 5 Geneva Street on land donated by Victor Hansen. It is still in use today. The firehouse was built by the men of the Fire Department and is still owned by them. The work to build the firehouse began in the fall of 1935.

The exterior of the building was faced with brick in keeping with the water works and sewer plant. The interior plans included a room for the heating plant, three stalls, and toilet facilities on the first floor and office space, a meeting room, and storage space located on the second floor

The members of the fire department took no pay for their services but rather donated the money from fire calls into a building fund. The Fire Department held events to raise funds for the fire station and for their much needed equipment.

Circa 1920s Early fund raising event sponsored by the Williams Bay Volunteer Fire Department. Photo credit: Tom and Kathy Leith.

Circa 1934 Water Barrel Fight between neighboring fire departments. Photo credit: Tom and Kathy Leith.

The department held its first Mid-Summer Carnival in 1934. The annual Mid-Summer Carnivals were supported by residents of the Village and friends of the Village from around the lake and helped to raise the additional funds needed to make the fire house a reality.

The carnivals were three-day events in July. Festivities included food, games, entertainment such as the local band and a parade with the Delavan Drum and Bugle Corps, and carnival rides. A highlight of the festivals were the Water Barrel Fights held each evening and on Sunday afternoon with fire departments from the neighboring towns.

Williams Bay's Volunteer Fire Department continues to serve all citizens of the village protecting property located in the village just as the founding members did in 1923.

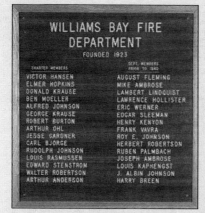

Members of the Williams Bay Fire Department: Founding members and members prior to 1940. Photo credit: Tom and Kathy Leith.

Circa 1938 Volunteer Fireman Ruben Palmbach in front of the firehouse at 5 Geneva Street. Photo credit: Barrett Memorial Library.

1932 Williams Bay Volunteer Fire Department outside of the Water Works building on Elkhorn Road (highway 67). Photo taken by George Blakslee. Photo credit: Terry Thomas Collection.

1927 Back row Left to Right: Lawrence A. Hollister; Ben Moeller, Rudolph Johnson, Victor Hansen, Lambert Lindquist, Henry Kenyon, Donald Krause, Edward Stenstrom, Edgar Sleeman.

Front row Left to Right: Alfred Johnson, Mike Ambrose, Walter Robertson, August Fleming, Eric Werner, George Krause, Louis Rasmussen, Joseph Ambrose, Oscar Stenstrom, Carl Osman.

Driver: F. Arthur Anderson.

Photo credit: Terry Thomas Collection.

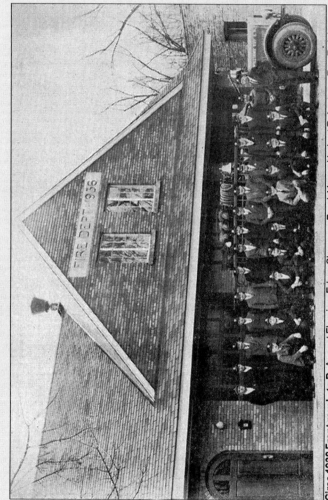

Circa 1938 Front row L. to R: August Fleming, Edgar Sleeman, Frank Vavra, Herbert Robertson, Roy E. Johnson, Edward Stenstrom, Henry Kenyon, Walter Robertson, Alfred Johnson.
Back row L to R: Chief Victor Hansen, Harry E. Breen, Lawrence A. Hollister, Carl M. Bjorge, Eric J. Werner, Arthur C. Ohl, Ben Moeller, Rudolph Johnson, Don Krause, Louis Kaphgenst, George Krause, F. Arthur Anderson, Mike Ambrose, Elmer H. Hopkins, Louis A. Rasmussen.   Photo credit: Barrett Memorial Library.

BREEZES FROM GENEVA LAKE

Here's to thee, O Fair Geneva!
We would oft thy praises sing,
Tribute bear in song and story
Till thy very woodlands ring.

Thine the oak crowned bluffs and hilltops,
Thine a hundred tangles dells,
And through many a charming vista
Babbling brooks thy glories tell.

O'er all they landscape peace is written,
Rest each shady lodge invites,
Music sweet thy waves are chanting,
Full and deep are thy delights.

So, Hail again, thou gem of beauty,
Sunlight on thy waters blue,
Flashes back, the heaven's glory,
Brings thy crystal depths to view.

When thy shores lie in deep shadow,
Fitting mirror of the night,
Moonlight on thy placid bosom
Gleams like Delphic water bright.

Then fare thee well, O, Dear Geneva!
Thou with rippling waters sweet,
Peace, till with the summer breezes
Once again thy shores we'll greet.

George C. Blakslee, 1892

Chapter 2

LAKEFRONT ACCESS

SHORE PATH/TRANSPORTATION/INDUSTRY

Circling Geneva Lake is a path that began with the first lake shore inhabitants. Early historical accounts make reference to a network of trails around the lake. The Potawatomi used these trails to travel from one village to another. Later this path would be used by local residents who worked at the grand estates surrounding the lake.

Geneva Lake is one of a very few developed lakes in America that has a public path along the shore for the entire distance around the lake. A treaty signed in 1833 guaranteed public access to the Lake Shore Path in perpetuity. At approximately 23 miles the shore path allows visitors and residents an opportunity to enjoy the beauty of the lake, the magnificence of the historic mansions, and meticulous landscaping designs by notable early landscape architects. Jens Jensen and the Olmstead Brothers left their imprint on the landscapes of Conference Point, Yerkes Observatory, Dronley, Wadsworth Hall, and other locations around the lake. A walk along the shore path will give you a glimpse of the history of the lake and the extravagant lifestyles of the early Chicago millionaires who arrived in Williams Bay on the Chicago & North Western train while their stately steam yachts waited at the pier to take them to their summer homes.

The resources and beauty of Geneva Lake would draw industry, businesses, and tourism to the area. People wanting to get away from the city life came to Geneva Lake by train, horse and buggy, and later automobiles and airplanes for rest and recreation. In the winters hundreds of men worked cutting ice to be stored in the ice houses in Williams Bay and Lake Geneva. In the summer train cars loaded with ice would be brought to Chicago and points beyond.

Circa 1920s View of Williams Bay looking at its western shore from the north. This shoreline has been home to a variety of camps, resorts, private residences, and associations, such as Conference Point, Congress Club, Rose Lane Resort, Sawyer's Cottages, Bay Shore Resort, and The Normandie Hotel. Photo Credit: Deborah Dumelle Kristmann Collection.

Circa 1910 Looking east toward Conference Point from the shoreline of the YMCA Camp. This area has been home to many of the popular summer camps: YMCA, Rockford Camp, Olivet Camp, Eleanor Camp, and Holiday Home. Photo credit: Deborah Dumelle Kristmann Collection.

Circa 1930s Looking north from the western shore toward the water tower and Chicago & North Western train station in Williams Bay. This view of a small section the Geneva Lake shore path was once part of the Potawatomi trail. The path hugs the shoreline for most of its 23 mile length and is accessible by law to the public which is a unique feature of Geneva Lake. Photo Credit: Deborah Dumelle Kristmann Collection.

Circa 1920s In the background the ice houses, water tower, piers, and many outbuildings of the train depot illustrate the development and many functions that took place at the head of the Bay. Photo Credit: Nancy Snidtker Baldwin.

1934 Bathing beach and Williams Bay lakefront. Photo credit: Rick Blakeley.

Circa 1925 Looking southeast at the early development of Cedar Point Park Association from Geneva Street which at the time hugged the shoreline. Photo Credit: Deborah Dumelle Kristmann Collection.

Circa 1930s Looking south from the head of the Bay along the shores of Cedar Point Park Association. Prior to being subdivided, the property was owned by Chicago businessman N. K. Fairbank, who also owned a lakeshore home on the north shore. The property was known as Fairbank's Woods and was a popular camping area for locals and tourists. Photo Credit: Deborah Dumelle Kristmann Collection.

CHICAGO & NORTH WESTERN RAILWAY

1890 The Railway depot in Williams Bay. Photo credit: Michelle Bie Love.

While the railroad first came to Lake Geneva (or Geneva as it was known in 1856), it would be only a few years until service was discontinued due the poor condition of the track. Rail service would come again to Lake Geneva on July 26, 1871.

By the mid 1880s Williams Bay was viewed as ready for railway expansion. The first proposal came in the fall of 1885, which suggested extending the line to Williams Bay and then to Delavan and Milton Junction. In 1886, another proposal suggested a line from Lake Geneva to Williams Bay for the summer resort trade and winter ice cutting.

With articles of association filed with the Wisconsin Secretary of State on August 5, 1887, the six mile stretch from Lake Geneva to Williams Bay was open for extension. Survey work had already been completed in the first half of June; the track would run a short distance north from the depot in Lake Geneva and turn west to follow the south shore of Duck Lake (Como). After crossing the Delavan Road (Highway 50) the track would make a sharp S curve south and then west to the lakefront in Williams Bay. Contracts had been

made with landowners by early July for the right of way.

Grade stakes were placed in early September and earthwork was started in mid-September with the grade ready for laying the track by mid-November. The new rail line was opened on June 1, 1888 with one train making the run to Williams Bay.

Albert Redfearn was the conductor on that first train to Williams Bay and Clyde Harrison was the first Station agent at the new depot. Most of the first passengers to Williams Bay had their own yachts waiting for them at the piers. Later the commercial steamers would carry passengers from the train to the resorts and camps around the lake.

Circa 1907 Conductor Albert Redfearn and Engineer George Murdock. Photo credit: Chicago Tribune.

1887 The Chicago & North Western Railroad extension from Lake Como to Williams Bay. Earthwork for laying the tracks from Lake Geneva to Williams Bay was begun in mid-September. Temporary housing structures were built for the men. In the early 1890s the railroad looked to improve conditions at the Williams Bay depot by filling in parts of the swampy land on the north side of the tracks. Photo credit: Deborah Dumelle Kristmann Collection.

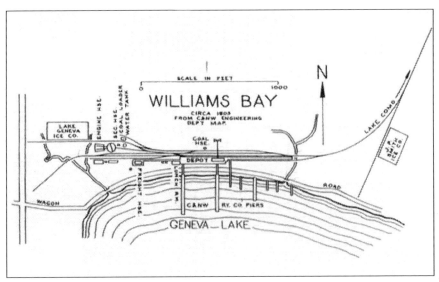

1905 Chicago & North Western Railway engineering map of the Williams Bay lakefront. Photo credit: Steam Trains to Geneva Lake: C&NW'S Elgin-Williams Bay by Paul L. Behrens.

Circa 1888-89 The first train pulled into Williams Bay on June 1, 1888. The 'period' after Williams Bay on the station sign denoted the end of the rail line from Chicago. In 1888 one train per day under the charge of conductor Albert Redfearn arrived in Williams Bay. Clyde Harrison was the first station agent. Photo credit: Walworth County Historical Society.

1895 With nearby accessibility to the lake and private yachts, Williams Bay provided a convenient alternative to accessing Geneva Lake for Chicagoans traveling to their summer homes, camps, and resorts. Smith Ice House is visible in the background. Photo credit: James Wallace Photo Collection, courtesy of Kate Morris Dickerson and Family.

Circa 1899 View of the train station and the west shore of Williams Bay from the northeast. On the right foreground is W. A. Lackey Lumber Yard. The large building in the background to the right is the Fernwood Inn owned by Eric Anderson. As you can tell by this photo, development of the village was just beginning. Photo credit: Terry Thomas Collection.

Circa 1910 Passenger train from Lake Geneva heading toward the end of the line in Williams Bay. In the background is Lake Como. Photo credit: Walworth County Historical Society.

Circa 1898 Passenger train waiting to leave for Lake Geneva and on to Chicago. Photo credit: Walworth County Historical Society.

1914 Chicago & North Western conductor at Williams Bay. A train left the Chicago & North Western Wells Street Station every day at 3:45 pm. On Friday a special train known as the "Millionaire's Special" left the Wells Street Station ahead of the regular commuter train. Photo credit: The United Church of Christ (Congregational) - Williams Bay.

CHICAGO & NORTH WESTERN'S MILLIONAIRES SPECIAL
WELLS STREET STATION TO WILLIAMS BAY

1907 The Millionaires Special departs the Wells Street Station for Lake Geneva and Williams Bay. Photo credit: Chicago Tribune.

The Chicago & North Western railway had a train leaving its Chicago Wells Street Station every week day at 3:45 pm for Williams Bay. On Friday a second train known as "Redfearn's Millionaire Mover" left the station first. Albert Redfearn was the conductor who had the distinction of knowing by name all the Chicago millionaires calling Geneva Lake their home.

From the polished trimmings of the fleet's iron horse, to the rear railing of the parlor car, the equipment of the 535 was luxurious in its modern make-up. The "Millionaires Special" went through towns, villages, and hamlets at 60 miles per hour, not stopping until it reached Lake

1907 Parlor cars of the Millionaires Special waiting for their precious freight. Photo credit: Chicago Tribune.

Geneva in a little over an hour and Williams Bay fifteen minutes later. The second train, the one with the common folks, made the trip to Williams Bay in about an hour and fifty minutes.

Private yachts belonging to millionaire businessmen from Chicago waited at the piers in Williams Bay to take them to their summer homes at the grand estates around the lake.

On any given Friday afternoon the seats of the parlor cars of the Millionaire Special were occupied by mostly self-made millionaires, who were bankers, judges, meat packers, manufacturers, retail magnets, lawyers, soap makers, professors, brewers, doctors, and members of the Chicago Board of Trade with names like: Allerton, Ayers, Bartlett, Beidler, Billings, Boyles, Chalmers, Chandler, Clowry, Cooke, Crane, Drake, Dunlap, Fairbank, Glennon, Grommes, Harbert, Harris, Hately, Healy, Hutchinson, Isham, Johnston, Jones, Keep, Leiter, Lefens, Lytton, McCrea, Mitchell, Moore, Parker, Potter, Rumsey, Ryerson, Sears, Seipp, Shaw, Smyth, Selfridge, Starring, Sturges, Swift, Swing, Ulhlein, Wacker, Walker, Weiss, Wetherall, Wheeler, Withrow, Wilmarth, and Young on their way to their palatial summer homes on the shore of Geneva Lake.

On one Friday afternoon in July 1907 40 millionaires boarded the 3:45 train to Lake Geneva and Williams Bay. According to calculations of wealth at the time, the net worth of these 40 millionaires was conservatively estimated to be $200 million. Calculating the value of a 1907 dollar to the value of a dollar today, those forty millionaires would have an estimated net worth of $5,224,862,886 in 2017.

Circa 1900 Private yachts waiting for their owners at the piers in Williams Bay. Photo credit: Deborah Dumelle Kristmann Collection.

Circa 1890 Engine 399 arriving in Williams Bay. In the background between the train and the depot is the Smith Ice House. To the left of the train is one of the many buildings that were used to store items which had arrived or were waiting to be shipped. Photo credit: Rick Blakeley.

Circa 1902 Passengers and a member of the train's crew waiting at the Williams Bay depot to board the train for Chicago. Photo credit: Nancy Snidtker Baldwin.

Circa 1900 Train arrival at the the Williams Bay station. Carriages and steamers waited for passengers. Photo credit: Rachel Gage, Pier 290, Gage Marine.

Circa 1930s Grover Spotz, a resident of Williams Bay and conductor for the Chicago & North Western Railway. Photo credit: Williams Bay Historical Society.

Circa 1910 Passengers arriving at Williams Bay. Many were probably arriving for vacations at one of the many camps or resorts around the lake or at their summer home on the lakeshore. Smith Ice House is visible behind the depot. Photo credit: Deborah Dumelle Kristmann Collection.

1914 One of the many men who worked at the depot to transport luggage or freight to or from the train. Photo credit: The United Church of Christ (Congregational) - Williams Bay.

Circa 1900 Williams Bay had three piers for steamers to dock and load or unload passengers. The piers were always bustling at train time. Photo credit: Barrett Memorial Library.

Circa 1915 Roundhouse in Williams Bay. The roundhouse was once an important building for railroads, allowing for the maintenance of locomotives. In the foreground is the turntable for turning locomotives so that they can be moved back in the direction from which they came. Photo credit: Walworth County Historical Society.

Circa 1915 Chicago & North Western water tower provided the water necessary for the steam engines. Photo credit: Walworth County Historical Society.

BOATS OPERATE ON STANDARD TIME WHICH IS ONE HOUR SLOWER THAN DAYLIGHT SAVING TIME

WISCONSIN TRANSPORTATION COMPANY

TEL. 35 LAKE GENEVA OFFICE   SUNDAY BOAT SCHEDULE   TEL. 120-W-1 WILLIAMS BAY

Stations (Read Down): Lake Geneva (Leave), Elgin Club, Williams Bay, Conference Point, Eleanor Camp, Olivet Camp, Holiday Home, Belvidere Club, Fontana, Glenwood Springs, Harvard Club, Chicago Club, N.W.M.&N. Academy, Country Club, South Shore Club, Lake Geneva (Arrive)

ROUND TRIP $1.00

Harvard Excursion Trip with Orchestra

The Management reserves right to change this schedule without notice.

WEEK DAY BOAT SCHEDULE

Stations (Read Down): Lake Geneva (Leave), Elgin Club, Williams Bay, Conference Point, Eleanor Camp, Y.M.C.A., Olivet Camp, Holiday Home, Belvidere Club, Fontana, Glenwood Springs, Harvard Club, Chicago Club, N.W.M.&N. Academy, Country Club, South Shore Club, Lake Geneva (Arrive)

All round trips via North Shore.

July 4th and Labor Day—Sunday Schedule

CHICAGO—LAKE GENEVA—
WILLIAMS BAY SERVICE (Via Wisconsin Div.)

NORTHBOUND	Nos. 517-755 Daily	No. 529 Except Sun.	Nos. 513-787 Except Sun.	No. 649 Except Sun.	Nos. 541-761 Except Sun.	No. 778 Sat. only	No. 771 Sun. only
	A. M.	A. M.	P. M.	P. M.	P. M.	A. M.	A. M.
Lv. Chicago	8.15	8.45	12.30	3.45	4.30	11.50	7.30
Lv. Crystal Lake	9.30	10.00	2.07		5.82		
Ar. Genoa City	10.14	10.43	2.51	5.27	6.35	1.25	9.10
Ar. Lake Geneva	10.34	10.59	3.06	5.32	6.47	1.41	9.26
Ar. Williams Bay	10.50	11.15	3.20	5.35	7.00	1.56	9.40

SOUTHBOUND	Nos.754-602 ExceptSun.	Nos.776-512 Sun. only	No. 664 ExceptSun.	Nos.738-508 ExceptSun.	No. 690 ExceptSun.	No. 770 Sun. only	Nos.766-746 Sun. only	No. 772 Sun. only	No.778 Mon. only
	A. M.	A. M.	A. M.	P. M.	P. M.	P. M.	P. M.	P. M.	A. M.
Lv. Williams Bay	5.35	6.15	6.50	4.05	8.00	†8.15	6.45	7.45	5.30
Lv. Lake Geneva	5.49	6.30	7.05	4.19	5.20	8.29	6.59	8.00	5.43
Lv. Genoa City	6.02	6.45	7.17	4.34	5.34		7.11	8.14	5.55
Lv. Crystal Lake	6.47	7.57		5.35			7.58		
Ar. Chicago	8.12	8.55	8.40	6.43	7.15	8.15	8.01	8.55	7.38

†Will not run on Sunday, May 30th (Memorial Day).

TRAIN SCHEDULE
Boats meet all Trains at Williams Bay.

TRAIN PICK UP
Passengers for 6.50 A.M. train leaving Williams Bay

AURORA—LEAVE

Glenwood Springs	6:00 A. M.
Fontana	6:05 A. M.
Belvidere Club	6:10 A. M.
Holiday Home	6:15 A. M.
Olivet Camp	6:15 A. M.
Y. M. C. A.	6:20 A. M.
Eleanor Camp	6:25 A. M.
Conference Point	6:30 A. M.
Williams Bay	6:35 A. M.

GENEVA—LEAVE

Harvard Club	5:55 A. M.
Chicago Club	6:05 A. M.
N. W. M. & N. Academy	6:25 A. M.
Williams Bay	6:35 A. M.

TRAINS

Passengers for	4.05 p.m.	5.00 p.m.	6.17 Sun. p.m.

AURORA—LEAVE

N.W.M.& N.Academy	2:15	3:45	4:40
Chicago Club	2:30	3:50	4:45
Harvard Club	2:30	4:05	4:55
Glenwood Springs	2:35	4:10	5:05
Fontana	2:40	4:15	5:10
Belvidere	2:45	4:20	5:15
Holiday Home	2:50	4:25	5:20
Oliver Camp	2:50	4:25	5:20
Y. M. C. A.	2:55	4:30	
Eleanor Camp	2:55	4:35	5:25
Conference Point	3:00	4:35	5:30
Williams Bay	3:10	4:45	5:40

The above boat schedules (circa 1926) show the close tie-in the steamboat lines had with the railroad.

1926 Schedules for Wisconsin Transportation Company and Chicago & North Western Railway. The schedules were carefully prepared to coordinate with the Chicago & North Western Railway trains at Lake Geneva and Williams Bay and with the electric cars at Fontana. Photo credit: Deborah Dumelle Kristmann Collection.

STEAM YACHTS

From the 1870s through the 1920s, dozens of elegant steam-powered yachts glided across the surface of Geneva Lake. The yachts would pick up their owners at the piers in Williams Bay when they arrived on the "Millionaire Special" at the train depot.

Owners would entertain guests, pick up friends for an afternoon of golf at Lake Geneva Country Club, or simply enjoy a quiet scenic cruise with family and friends. This was an era of elegance, when the extravagant homes of Chicago's millionaires graced the shoreline of Geneva Lake.

When the Chicago & North Western rail line from Lake Geneva to Williams Bay was completed in 1888, it was only a short walk from the club-car equipped train to the waiting yachts at the municipal piers. Yachts with polished brass, glistening varnish, rich appointments, and captains dressed in uniforms made a fine sight on the lakefront.

Today, only a handful of the elegant yachts remain. They are lovingly maintained and cared for by their owners who cherish their rich history on Geneva Lake.

Circa 1915 Elegant yachts await their owner's arrival on the "Millionaire Special" and chauffeured cars and buggies await other passengers arriving at the station. From one of the Wisconsin Transportation Company brochures: "Wisconsin Transportation Company operated one of the finest equipped inland lake lines in the country. Making both leisurely and fast close-to-shore trips affording a close-up panorama of the magnificent residences and their grounds and the wonderful scenic beauty bordering America's greatest lake." Photo credit: Deborah Dumelle Kristmann Collection.

Circa 1906 Yachts from lakeside estates and resorts at the docks in Williams Bay waiting for their owner's families and guests arriving from Chicago. Photo credit: Deborah Dumelle Kristmann Collection.

Circa 1890s Steamers and row boats await passengers at the lakefront in Williams Bay. Photo credit: Barrett Memorial Library.

Circa 1890s Steamers Majestic and Commodore docked in Williams Bay. Photo credit: Barrett Memorial Library.

Circa 1910 Wisconsin Transportation Company's Harvard cruised the shoreline showing visitors places of interest every Sunday afternoon at 2 pm from Lake Geneva. An orchestra furnished music for this trip. Photo credit: Deborah Dumelle Kristmann Collection.

Circa 1910 The Louise owned by the Wisconsin Transportation Company took passengers around Geneva Lake. Today, the Louise is owned by Gage Marine and is still carrying passengers on tours of the lake. Photo Credit: Michelle Bie Love.

Circa 1905 The steamer Passaic owned by Richard Teller Crane. In 1880 the Crane's first steam yacht Passaic arrived on Geneva Lake serving the family until 1899. The Crane's second Passaic was launched in 1899. Mr. Crane frequently cruised around the lake picking up his friends for a game of golf at Lake Geneva Country Club. In 1890 the first Passaic was sold to William J. Chalmers, less than a week after his steam yacht Thistle burned and sank. Mr. Chalmers was the owner of Dronley estate, on the western shore of Williams Bay. After the Chalmers left the lake in 1918 their yacht was brought to Delavan Lake where she remained for a short time and renamed the Delavan. In 1949 the yacht was purchased by Russell and Bill Gage who lovingly restored her to her former elegance, the steamer was rechristened the Matriark. Photo credit: Williams Bay Historical Society.

Circa 1920s The Aurora approaching pier in Williams Bay. Length: 62 feet; weight: approx. 60 tons. Photo credit Barrett Memorial Library.

Circa 1930s: Williams Bay residents worked for the Wisconsin Transportation company. Front Row: Jerry Thornley, Tom Murphy, and Sam Thornley (Capt. of the Aurora). Back Row: Phil Fogle, George Woods, Louis Anderson, Howie Olson, and Hal Iverson. Photo credit: Barrett Memorial Library.

HORSE AND BUGGY

Before the automobile, and even for many years after its invention, some residents of Williams Bay and the surrounding area relied on the horse and buggy or wagon for transportation.

Early roads were little more than the dirt paths left by the Potawatomi and many were almost impassable after a heavy rain, When winter snow melted the thin tires of early automobiles would become stuck in the mud while horses could pull a buggy or wagon through the quagmire.

1914 Geneva Street with the Library in the background. The Hollister residence is in the background on the right. Photo credit; The United Church of Christ (Congregational) - Williams Bay.

1914 Lackey driveway on Clover Street. Photo credit: The United Church of Christ (Congregational) - Williams Bay.

1914 Horses were used by farmers to work their fields and as transportation into town for supplies. Photo credit: The United Church of Christ (Congregational) - Williams Bay.

1914 Buggies came in many different styles from two-wheel carts to elaborate carriages. Prized horses of every shape and color were stabled in barns throughout the Village. Here Mae Lyndon is out for a drive. Photo credit: The United Church of Christ (Congregational) - Williams Bay.

Automobiles

Development and maintenance of roads in Wisconsin remained a low priority in the early twentieth century despite the number of automobiles that were being produced. The most popular mode of travel continued to be by rail resulting in funding going for additional rail lines.

The purpose of the Good Roads Movement was the improvement of roads but was mostly aimed at helping farmers get their wagons to market rather than helping automobiles maneuver the same poor road conditions. In 1911 the State Aid Road Law was passed and Wisconsin's roads began to be paved with gravel. The State Highway Commission saw the need for improved roads for automobile travel in 1916 and the following year a system of highways began to be established throughout the

state. As road conditions improved, more people were able to travel by automobile and slowly their dependence on rail travel declined.

Improved roads allowed the automobile to play a major part in Wisconsin's growing economy. The automobile presented new opportunities to Wisconsinites, transforming their daily life with access to new job opportunities and a growing tourism industry statewide.

In 1905 H. Sargent Michaels published travel guides for motorists. Instead of the maps we know today, the guide included pictures and descriptions of corners and locations along the travel route.

1914 The first automobiles appeared around 1900. At first people did not think of them as something useful; they were more like toys. Photo credit: The United Church of Christ (Congregational) - Williams Bay.

1914 Boys and girls who grew up when the first autos came into use, learned to drive at an early age. Some were only 11 or 12 years old. There was less concern about serious accidents then because cars did not go very fast and there were so few of them on the road. Photo credit: The United Church of Christ (Congregational) - Williams Bay.

1914 Early cars were expensive and unreliable. They always seemed to be breaking down, and tires went flat as often as once or twice a day on an all-day trip! Photo credit: The United Church of Christ (Congregational) - Williams Bay.

Circa 1930 Wib Johnson - "No Autos allowed on Park or Line to Pier." Photo credit: Catzy and Julie Johnson.

1905 Delap's Corner (Highways 50 and 67) Looking east. Road to Williams Bay is on the right. To the left is the road to Elkhorn. Road straight ahead went to Lake Geneva. Guide description of corner: "For Williams Bay - White cottage on left, red shed on right setting flush with road." Photo credit: 1905 H. Sargent Michaels Guide for Motorist.

1905 Delap's Corner (Highways 50 and 67) Looking west Road to Williams Bay is on the left. To the right is the road to Elkhorn. Road straight ahead went to Delavan. Guide description of corner: "For Williams Bay - White cottage on right, red shed on left setting flush with road." Photo credit: 1905 H. Sargent Michaels Guide for Motorist.

Circa 1936 Gas station at Vitkus Corner (Highway 50 and Geneva Street). Photo credit: Grassroots Lake Geneva, Phil Fogle.

Circa 1920s Gena Dell ready to go for a ride on Walworth Avenue. Photo credit: Nancy Snidtker Baldwin.

DARING YOUNG MEN IN THEIR FLYING MACHINES

Before World War I, planes were rare and one was lucky to have seen one. Pilots who returned from the "war to end all wars" supported themselves by traveling around the country to small towns to show off their flying skills, as well as to take paying passengers for rides. A farm paddock or fair ground with sufficient room to take off and land was enough for these early "barnstormers" as they were called.

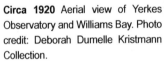

Circa 1920 aeroplane "Geneva" at the observatory Flying Field at Williams Bay. Photo Credit: Deborah Dumelle Kristmann Collection.

Circa 1920 Aerial view of Yerkes Observatory and Williams Bay. Photo credit: Deborah Dumelle Kristmann Collection.

Circa 1930s Pontoon planes would land on Geneva Lake, bringing tourists to resorts and camps or residents to their lakeshore homes. Photo credit: Deborah Dumelle Kristmann Collection.

'GOOD-BYE' WAS TRUE WORD FOR PLANE VICTIM

Miss Edith Gates of Williams Bay, Wis. told her friends good-bye before starting on fateful airplane ride with fiancé as pilot.

A girl and her fiancé were killed yesterday when an airplane in which they were flying between Elkhorn and Williams Bay took a nose-dive and plunged 1000 feet to the ground. The victims were Edith Gates, 19, of Williams Bay and Cyrill Burton, owner and pilot of the plane.

An uncle of the dead girl Frank Gates, a farmer living near Elkhorn, saw the tragedy from the back porch of his house. The plane had been circling over the Gates farm and he was waiting for it to land.

It is reported that Burton had been endeavoring to get Miss Gates to go up with him all summer but that she had refused. Yesterday, however, she consented to his request. Before going up she told all her friends good-bye, and the farewell proved to be her very last words to them.

All summer young Burton and his partner, Robert Ellis of Chicago, had operated the plane an old prewar model of the type known as "Jenny" (similar to the plane shown above) as commercial pilots, soliciting passengers from among the tourists at Lake Geneva. They had no flying license declared officials last night. Burton and Ellis stored their plane on the farm of Miss Gates' father, Harry Gates, at Williams Bay and it was in this way that the doomed love affair started. Friends said they were expected to wed soon.

After beginning yesterday's flight the plane showed indications of trouble and shortly before the crash Burton had made a landing for repairs. Taking off again, the plane had been under way only a few minutes when the engine stopped and the plane took its fatal nose-dive.

The bodies of the young victims were taken to undertaking rooms at Elkhorn where an inquest was held today.

Miss Gates graduated only last year from Williams Bay High School. She is survived by her parents, Harry and Mabel Gates, and siblings Donald, Raymond, and Doris.

Reprinted from the Republican North Western, Friday, July 27, 1928.

1928 Plane crash that killed Edith Gates and her fiancé Cyril Burton. Photo credit: Terry Thomas Collection.

ICE HARVESTING

Ice harvesting was a colorful and exciting enterprise. The workers dressed heavily and wore Scotch caps to protect their ears from the cold winter winds. They spoke a now-long-forgotten language as they called directions to their fellow workers.

Ice was harvested when the ice was at least two feet thick. A large rectangle was marked off into cakes two feet by four feet. First a hole was made in the ice, then horse-drawn plows would cut the ice along the lines in one direction and then the other. Workers would break off the ice cakes with saws and picks which were then stored in ice houses. Sawdust was packed between the cakes and when the ice house was full, the cakes of ice were covered with coarse hay that was cut for that purpose. This hay came from marshes around Horicon, Waukau, Monches, and Green Bay.

Ice harvesting was big business in the 19th and early 20th centuries until iceboxes were replaced by mechanical refrigeration in homes and businesses across America.

Circa 1900 Large rectangles of ice were marked off and cut by horse-drawn plows. the harvested ice was moved in troughs to the Knickerbocker or Smith Bros ice houses where it was stacked and stored, waiting to be shipped in refrigerated train cars to Chicago and points beyond. Photo credit: *Ice and Refrigeration,* A Monthly Review of the Ice, Ice Making, Refrigerating, Cold Storage, and kindred Trades, Vol. XIII No. 5 (1897)

Circa early 1900s Workers moving cakes of ice on Southwick Creek to the Knickerbocker Ice House. Photo credit: Barrett Memorial Library.

1920s Rooming house for ice workers at the Ambrose Ice House on Elkhorn Road. The kitchen and dining room were on the first floor and more than 50 ice house workers slept in bunks on the second and third floors. Later the house had apartments for two families. The house was burned for a fire fighting training exercise on May 25, 1968. Photo credit: John A. Anderson.

1897 The Smith Brother's Ice House after fire destroyed the warehouse. Ironically, thousands of tons of ice, packed in coarse marsh hay, remained after the fire. Note the box car on the far right for scale. Photo Credit: Barrett Memorial Library.

Ice Cutting Tools

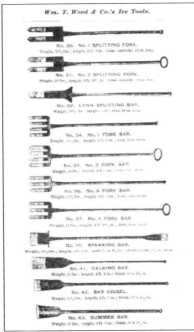

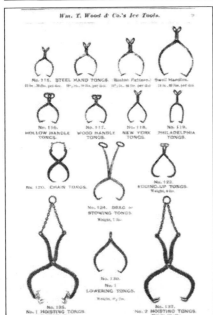

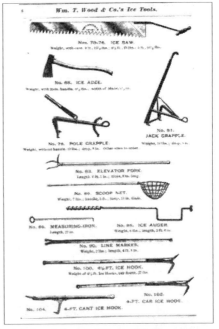

Circa 1894 Ice cutting tools from the Wm. T. Wood & Co., Arlington, MA. In 1905 the company was consolidated with Gifford Brothers of Hudson, NY, as Gifford-Wood Co. Photo credit: Davistown Museum - Ice Tools, Davistown, MA.

Chapter 3

A HERITAGE OF YEAR - ROUND RECREATION

BOATING/SWIMMING/FISHING/SAILING

Geneva Lake was the playground of Chicagoans and locals alike beginning as early as the 1870s. Williams Bay had abundant opportunities for recreation in every season.

In the spring and summer, boating, fishing, swimming, and sailing brought people to Geneva Lake. Golfing and horseback riding as well as badminton and tennis were enjoyed by locals and visitors to the lake. Friday evening movies at the park or school brought families together for an evening of fun.

Fall and winter offered just as many activities for enthusiasts. Hunting was a popular hobby of many men and the village even had a Rod and Gun Club. The Village and the Chicago & North Western railroad offered a special Sunday train in the winter called the "Snow Train." This train brought passengers to Williams Bay to ski at the village ski hill, or to iceboat, ice fish, and ice skate on the lake. Even sulky or harness races were held on the lake.

Winter, spring, summer, and fall Williams Bay had activities for the entire family to enjoy.

Circa 1910 Winter sports enthusiasts found an opportunity to iceboat and ice skate as well as to try their luck at catching that big fish on Geneva Lake. Photo credit: Deborah Dumelle Kristmann Collection.

SPRING AND SUMMER

Circa 1930s W. D. Denton Boat Livery. The livery rented row and motor boats. The livery also offered guide services to fishermen. Pictured are William D. Denton, Dewey Denton, and unknown man. Photo credit Barrett Memorial Library.

Circa 1920s View of the municipal pier in Williams Bay. Photo credit Barrett Memorial Library.

Circa 1930s From his pier and building on the lakefront, Victor Hansen, proprietor of Hansen Boat Company, sold gasoline and bait, rented boats to fisherman on Geneva Lake. Hansen Boat Company also provided guide services to fishermen. In addition to the services provided to fishermen, Hansen Boat Company serviced, repaired, and stored boats for local fishermen and boating enthusiasts. Mel Hansen and his wife Lillian would continue to operate the Livery on the lakefront until the Village of Williams Bay decided to renovate the lakefront in the 1970s. Photo credits: Tom and Kathy Leith.

Circa 1930s Victor Hansen was an active participant in many areas of life in the Village, Fire Chief, proprietor of Hansen's Pier, Village Trustee, and County Supervisor. Photo credit: Tom and Kathy Leith.

Circa 1920s A good day fishing. Photo credit: Barrett Memorial Library.

Circa 1920s Richard Snidtker and Grace Snidtker with their mother Gena Dell. Fishing was enjoyed by all members of the family. Notice the Knickerbocker Ice House and the rail yard in the background. Photo credit: Nancy Snidtker Baldwin.

THE STORY OF THE CISCO

Circa 1920 Cisco fishing on Williams Bay. Photo credit: Deborah Dumelle Kristmann Collection.

"The residents around Geneva Lake justly pride themselves in possessing a fish of unique character, superlative flavor, and of unusually erratic habits. For one week in June, cisco fishing in Geneva Lake is a great attraction. The cisco is a fresh-water herring which is found in great numbers during this particular season, attracted by swarms of sand-flies also found at this time in the summer. After the week the ciscos disappear for another year.

The cisco is an exceptionally colored fish, with a metallic sheen of mingled green, blue, and rose tints above the lateral line, and silver sides glowing in lustre equal to that of the molten metal on the tarpon, the acrobat of the Southern Seas.

The flavor of the cisco's flesh, flaky and creamy, is peculiarly sweet and appetizing, and can only be described by calling it of cisco savor, for no other fish has such a characteristic and pleasing taste. It commands during the season one dollar per pound, an equal price with that of the brook trout, the fad fish of the aristocrat's table, which unlike the cisco, is only fine in flavor when cooked later. The Geneva Lake fish runs almost mathematically uniform in size, ten to eleven inches, thus differing from those of its kind found in other waters."

Western Summer Resorts,
July 13, 1876

Circa 1920s Cisco washed up on lake shore. Photo Credit: Tom and Kathy Leith.

Circa 1930s The Margaret is decked out and ready to take guests on the lake for a sunset cruise. Photo Credit: Nancy Snidtker Baldwin.

Circa 1890s A peaceful Sunday afternoon rowing on Williams Bay. In the background are the piers where steam yachts picked up passengers arriving on the Chicago & North Western train across the road. Photo credit: Nancy Snidtker Baldwin.

Circa 1925 William Snidtker in his boat on Williams Bay. Notice the buildings in the background. Knickerbocker Ice house on the left and the buildings used by the railroad and businesses that shipped or received goods via train. Photo credit: Nancy Snidtker Baldwin.

Circa 1930s Williams Bay Lakefront at the Southwick Creek inlet. Looking east at the boat liveries that once dotted the shoreline. In the background is Cedar Point. Photo credit: Williams Bay Historical Society.

Circa 1930s Victor Hansen at the municipal pier helping launch a cabin cruiser that had been stored across the road on land rented from the Chicago & North Western Railroad. Note the double axle trailer with wood spoked wheels. Photo credit: Tom and Kathy Leith.

Circa 1930s A variety of wooden boats could be found on Geneva Lake. Visitors could take a ride on a famed Gar Wood at Moeller's Speed and Sail Boat Taxi in Williams Bay. Gar Wood boats were built by the famed Garfield Wood. Garfield Wood was the first man to travel over 100 mph on water. Photo Credit: Deborah Dumelle Kristmann Collection.

Circa early 1900s Victorian-style bathing suits were quite heavy and cumbersome. Made of wool they were meant to cover the body to retain modesty. Photo credit: Nancy Snidtker Baldwin.

Circa early 1900s Row boat racing was an early sport on lakes around the world and became an Olympic summer sport game in 1896. Possibly inspired by the Columbian Regatta which was held at Geneva Lake in 1893. Photo credit: Nancy Snidtker Baldwin.

Circa 1930s Guri and Martha Bergesen are ready for a dip in the Bay. Photo credit: Guri Henderson.

Circa 1905 William P. Snidtker, Williams Bay resident and chauffeur for Richard Teller Crane owner of the estate Jerseyhurst and founder of Crane Company and John Tilbern (another Crane chauffeur) hanging out on the pier with Charlie Crane, grandson of Richard Teller Crane. Photo credit: Nancy Snidtker Baldwin.

Circa 1920s Williams Bay Beach. The swimming pier was large and came out from the shore. When people walking out onto the pier caused it to become too crowded, the decision to remove several feet of the pier from the shoreline solved the problem. Photo credit: Deborah Dumelle Kristmann Collection.

Circa 1920s Richard (Dick) Snidtker aquaplaning (standing on a board while being pulled by a power boat) in the Bay. Aquaplaning was the predecessor to water skiing which was Invented by Ralph Wilford Samuelson in 1922 at Lake Pepin and first performed in Lake City, Minnesota. Photo credit: Nancy Snidtker Baldwin.

Circa 1920s The YMCA Kish-Wau-Ke-Toe Golf Club was later called George Williams Golf Course. Dr. Edwin Frost, an astronomer at Yerkes Observatory, was instrumental in the establishment of the golf course. Photo credit: Deborah Dumelle Kristmann Collection.

Circa 1930s Club House at George Williams Golf Course. Dr. Frost was the first winner of the Spaulding Cup at George Williams Golf Course. Photo credit: Deborah Dumelle Kristmann Collection.

Circa 1890s Family camping; perhaps it was cooler to sleep in the tent on hot summer nights than the house in the background or a "guest room" for visiting family or friends. Photo credit: Deborah Dumelle Kristmann Collection.

Circa 1890s Area residents and visitors enjoyed camping and picnicking near the shores of Geneva Lake. Family members from the littlest child to grandma and grandpa enjoyed getting away from the city to camp and enjoy the fresh country air. Campers were drawn to the scenic beauty of Geneva Lake. Fairbank's Woods was an especially popular location for camping and picnics for local residents. Photo credit: A John Bullock photo part of the Deborah Dumelle Kristmann Collection.

Circa 1920s Horseback riding was a popular past time in Williams Bay. In the 1930s there were two riding stables located within the village limits: Kenyon's Stable and Dick Horlick's Riding Academy. Photo credit: Nancy Snidtker Baldwin.

Circa 1930s Residents as well as people staying in the hotels and resorts in Williams Bay were able to go to the Riding Academy for riding lessons. Photo credit: Bay Leaves.

GENEVA LAKE WATER SAFETY PATROL

Geneva Lake Water Safety Patrol originated in 1920 with posters providing water safety information.

The annual Red Cross Institute under the supervision of Captain J. S. Law met at Conference Point in 1925; The Lake Geneva Chapter assisted by Mr. S. B. Chapin promoted the work of the Red Cross, promoted Mr. Wendell Berger Director of the chapter.

Mr. Wendell was assisted by 12 paid Life Guards at the different beaches and camps. Volunteer Guards who passed the American Red Cross Life Saving Test assisted the Life Guards. Two thousand hours of volunteer service was reported.

In 1925 there were 280 piers around the lake and swimming was indulged in at 98% of them. During that season 558 beginners and swimmers were examined and received Red Cross buttons. Mr. Wendell tested 166 junior and senior life savers. Seven demonstrations were given to 1,450 people during the season.

The Williams Bay Public Beach, Conference Point, Eleanor Camp, YMCA College Camp, Olivet Camp, Holiday Home were among the many beaches and camps around the lake benefited from this service. The actual cost for the service was $1,853 which included the salaries life guards. Materials and boat upkeep including the Director's salary was $966.

Countless lives have been saved by the Geneva Lake Water Safety Patrol since 1925.

1925 Safety Patrol boat, Director and Patrons of the Red Cross Safety Plan. Photo credit: Picturesque Lake Geneva, Bonnie Burton Denison, Wisconsin Transportation Company.

Circa 1920s Simeon B. Chapin, along with other lake residents, saw a need for an organization that was dedicated to spreading the word about the importance of safety through posters and bulletins posted at area beaches. Incidences of drowning were an all too common occurrence on the lake. The first members of the safety patrol were swim instructors who offered free swimming lessons at various locations around the lake.

By 1925, the Water Safety Patrol began providing lifeguards at Geneva Lake beaches and the organization purchased its first Patrol boat. The boat was used to expand the lifeguard services and provide assistance and rescue to an increasing number of boaters on the lake each summer. The Water Safety Patrol was first based in a small shed at the Riviera Pier. Photo credit: Picturesque Lake Geneva.

Circa 1930s Williams Bay Beach with one of the Water Safety Patrol boats waiting on shore. Photo credit: The Morava Family.

106

Circa 1930s Geneva Lake Water Safety Patrol
Front row Left to Right: F. Durkee, R. Mann, R. Nielsen, W. Smith (Lake Geneva), R. Paterson, N. Paterson (all points), W. Netz, J. Brugger, W. Hammersley, C. Lenon (Lake Geneva). **Second row Left to Right:** J. Tuchlinsky (Lake Geneva), M. McKenzie (Cedar Point Park), M. Finer (Lake Geneva Club), M. Featherstone (Fontana), S.B. Chapin - founder, W. Williams, H. Hemphill, R. Sweet (Eleanor Camp), G. Rand (Highlands), S. Craig (Olivet Camp). **Third row Left to Right:** E. Stone (Fontana), W. Tuchlinsky, H. Wells (Lake Geneva), R. Wright (Buena Vista Park), R. Fast (College Camp), E. Williams (Olivet Camp), R. Snidker (Williams Bay), D. Davidson, S.L. Gault (Holiday Home), T. Brugger (Lake Geneva), H.C. Patterson - Director, Wesley Severance (Hebron Camp). **Back row Left to Right:** E. Zingle, J. Rome (Buttons Bay), C. Parker (Buena Vista Park), Wesley Stoneburner, L.R. Wharry, J. Marley (College Camp), M. Stenstrom, D. Van Epps (Williams Bay), F. Dill, R. Fels (Conference Point). Photo credit: Nancy Snidtker Baldwin.

Circa 1930s Grace Snidtker by the family cottage on Walworth Avenue. The first members of the Water Safety Patrol were swimming instructors. Photo credit: Nancy Snidtker Baldwin.

GENEVA LAKE YACHT CLUB

The Geneva Lake Yacht Club (as it was initially known) was begun in 1874 with the first Sheridan Prize Race. The race was held in honor of visiting Lieutenant General Philip Sheridan. The Lake Geneva Herald reported the victory of the Nettie owned by Julian S. Rumsey, Mayor of Chicago (1861-1862) and seasonal resident, was greeted with "great cheering by friends and screeching steam whistles."

On April 29, 1876, a group of sailing enthusiasts, including A. C. Calkins, Al Lytle, George L. Dunlap, General A. C. Ducat, John Bullock, John W. French, Julian S. Rumsey, and N. K. Fairbank met at the Whiting House Hotel to adopt the bylaws and constitution of the club and to establish the rules governing future races. The group also recognized August 31, 1874, the date of the first Sheridan Prize race, as the founding date of the club. For the first 32 years of its existence the club would have no home.

In 1902 representatives of the Geneva Lake Yacht Club and the West End Yacht Club, located in Fontana, agreed to merge and named the new club the Lake Geneva Yacht Club. The goal of the new club was to establish a permanent location

In 1906, with the membership numbering more than 100, members built their first clubhouse, leasing property at the tip of Cedar Point for $500 per year from Kellogg Fairbank. Fairbank had been the club's commodore in 1890 and was the son of the club's first commodore, N. K. Fairbank. The Cedar Point clubhouse was an attractive two-story building with a wide veranda, set among trees.

A few years later club members registered some concerns about the terms of the lease and by the time it expired in 1916, Mr. Fairbank chose not to renew it. Once again the yacht club was homeless.

1906 Geneva Lake Yacht Club pier at Cedar Point. Photo credit: Lake Geneva Yacht Club.

1906 The clubhouse was built and ready for the summer of 1906. A simple building with wide front steps and generous verandas, it had a reception room and offered some sleeping accommodations for members and their guests. In 1916, thinking of the future development of Cedar Point Mr. Fairbank refused to renew the Yacht Club's lease. The members wanted to move their clubhouse across the ice to a new location but Mr. Fairbank would not let them cut down any trees. Photo credits: Deborah Dumelle Kristmann Collection.

1906 The Lake Geneva Yacht Club pier at Cedar Point. One of the most popular early sailing yachts were called Sandbaggers; which had a wide beam and open, shallow draft. They carried 50 pound sand bags as a ballast that were shifted windward by the crew with every tack. Photo Credit: Lake Geneva Yacht Club.

Circa 1914 Sailing in the Sheridan Race. In 1872 the Geneva Regatta Club was organized; it was the first group on the lake for the purpose of rowing and sailing. Its bylaws were fairly strict and indicated that the membership experience would be similar to that of joining the Navy. With limited participation the organization only lasted two years. Photo Credit: Deborah Dumelle Kristmann Collection.

Circa 1912 The Yacht Club fleet getting ready to race. Photo credit: Deborah Dumelle Kristmann Collection.

Circa 1908 Lake Geneva Yacht Club pier. Sailing in 1906 was in four classes, designated by size as A, B, C, and D, and the club held some big regattas in those early years, most importantly the North-western Regatta Association's events in 1906, 1907, and 1908. In 1906, the regatta attracted more than 50 boats. Photo credit: Deborah Dumelle Kristmann Collection.

FALL AND WINTER

Circa 1925 Showing off the day's hunt at Hopkins and Walker Garage. During the late 1800s and early 1900s, market hunters relentlessly pursued waterfowl from early fall through late spring virtually everywhere the birds congregated in large numbers. Alarmed by the decline of waterfowl populations, sportsmen pressed the federal government to regulate waterfowl harvests. In 1918, the U.S. Congress passed the Migratory Bird Treaty Act. The legislation established the first federal bag limits for waterfowl, protected threatened species and banned market hunting, spring shooting, and the use of shotguns larger than 10 gauge. Photo credit: Carl Hanley.

1919 Author and sportsman the Reverend Paul Burrill Jenkins and his son after a hunting trip. Paul Jenkins was an expert marksman and a firearms expert; was one of the curators of the collection of firearms at the Milwaukee Public Museum. Photo credit: American Magazine January 1920.

Circa 1925 Sledding was enjoyed by boys and girls in Williams Bay. Photo credit: Grandpa's Big Book-Carol Stenstrom Ortiz.

Circa 1925 A heavy wet snow was good for packing and a day full of fun. The possibilities were endless; snow men, snow angels, snow forts, snowball fights, sledding and home-made toboggan runs. Enterprising kids built snow tunnels and jumps to make sledding and tobogganing more exciting. Photo credit: Grandpa's Big Book-Carol Stenstrom Ortiz.

MEMORIES OF A YOUNG LAD IN THE BAY - MID 1920S

Easily the most vivid memory of my youth in The BAY is the occasional opportunity to join in a ride through the center of town on a large Bobsled built and owned by Piehl's Lumber Yard. This sled was 'No Toy'—large enough to carry 8-10 young children plus the two adults required to handle the long and heavy sled, one adult to steer using a level steering wheel and another at the rear of the sled to operate the manual brakes. One long board ran the length of the sled as did foot rests on either side. One's first impression of this "toy" was of its length and weight.

I don't believe any of we younger ones gave any thought to the possible danger involved in our moments of fear-fun! As I look back...ANY sort of crash at speed would have been a disaster but then youth is spared these fears.

The ride would follow this sequence: Locate the town constable and get his approval for the run(s). Locate two adult size men to operate the sled. Easiest chore, find about ten children to take the ride. Then, and only then, would Piehl's Lumber Yard release the sled and we'd all pitch in to haul it up the hill until we were even with the entrance to Yerkes Observatory.

ALL ABOARD! And we slowly began the ride down the hill —picking up speed that most certainly exceeded ANYTHING else traveling our streets. When we reached a point about opposite Southwick's Hardware Store, which was the building just across from the library, we'd all scream at the top of our lungs and in a flash we'd round the slight bend and drop at our highest speed, right through the center of town, passing the constable who'd stopped any traffic present, usually horse and wagons. Then we'd leave the road and cut through the park and out onto the ice-covered bay waters. A good driver would have us stopped on the far side against Cedar Point Park near the road. If agreed upon we'd do 'er again or others could claim a ride, fair is fair—NO argument!

To this day, I've NEVER, EVER had a more exciting ride! My first was probably in 1929-30! The terrible speed coupled with the growl of the heavy runners on the snow and ice couldn't be duplicated, you'd hafta ride it!

Warren Thornley in his 82nd year - 2004

Circa 1925 Peter Stenstrom and his son Oscar taking a ride on their bobsled. Photo credit: Grandpa's Big Book-Carol Stenstrom Ortiz.

1910 Members of the Yerkes Observatory ski club crossing country skiing on the grounds of the Observatory. Edward E. Barnard is on the left. Photo credit: Williams Bay Alumni Association and Yerkes Observatory.

Circa 1924 "Ski jumping is coming back to the territory. A group of young businessmen headed by Carl Bjorge, Frank Walker, and J. Jorgenson have constructed a jump at Stams Park near Yerkes Observatory. Winter sports are growing here and on Geneva Lake due to efforts of boosters." (Janesville Daily Gazette - January 28, 1924) Photo credit: Grandpa's Big Book-Carol Stenstrom Ortiz.

Circa 1924 Skiing was a popular winter sport for Williams Bay residents of all ages Photo credit: Grandpa's Big Book-Carol Stenstrom Ortiz.

Circa 1924 Teenage boy cross country skiing to his favorite hunting spot. Photo credit: Grandpa's Big Book-Carol Stenstrom Ortiz.

116

Circa 1930s Ski Jump at the Bay ski hill. Each winter for many years the Snow Train would bring passengers from Chicago to Williams Bay to enjoy the many winter sports available to them: ice boating, skiing, tobogganing, and skating. Carl Bjorge taught many Williams Bay youngsters to ski on this hill. Photo credit: Jim Moeller.

Ski-Ball The New Hot Beverage
From the February 18, 1937 issue of Bay Leaves. "Ski-Ball parties are quite the rage among snow and ice lovers."

How to make a Ski-Ball
Use a mug with a handle. Place one and half teaspoon of sugar in the bottom of the mug. Put 12 large or 18 small whole cloves in a quarter inch slice of lemon and place on top of sugar in mug. Next place a cinnamon stick in the mug that is long enough to be used as a muddler. Steep one teaspoon of black tea for each cup of boiling water for five minutes exactly.
Pour into prepared mug and enjoy!

Circa 1937 Ski hill and warming shack. Painting by Ed Elsner Sr. In the background is the Oscar Palm farm (Oscar Palm was the father of Ethel Weith who owned the Arctic Circle Drive Inn and lived in the homestead with her husband Albert and their family.) Further back is the farm of William Southwick and his son Ernest. The Southwick farm was founded in the 1840s by William's father. (Ernest Southwick was the father of Mary Ingersoll who lived in the family homestead, founded in the 1840s, with her husband John and their family.) Photo credit: Joan Elsner Miller.

Circa 1930s Skiers at the Bay ski hill use the tow rope installed by Carl Bjorge to get back to the top of the hill. Photo credit: Terry Thomas Collection.

Circa 1924 Ice fishing at Williams Bay Photo credit: Barrett Memorial Library.

Circa 1930s During the hey-day of steam yachts docking in Williams Bay there were three municipal piers across from the train station. The longest pier was about 250 feet long and 20 feet wide and covered with a substantial roof for most of its length. These piers were probably the strongest on the lake, staying in the lake throughout the winter. Photo credit: Williams Bay Historical Society.

Circa 1920s The first iceboats were adaptations of regular sailing boats, with a wooden plank fastened cross-wise at the front with a fixed runner at each end, and a steering runner attached to the bottom of the rudder at the stern. The traditional stern-steerer boats were largely replaced by front steering boats in the 1930s. Photo credit: Williams Bay Historical Society.

Circa 1920s Ray Moeller and ice boat. Chicago & North Western water tower is in the background. Photo credit: Jim Moeller.

Circa 1920s "Stern-steerer" iceboats were generally rigged as sloops, with a jib sail forward of the mast, although the catboat style with a single sail was also used. These early ice sailing vessels led to the development of boats designed strictly for racing on ice. While the large stern-steerers could have up to 600 square feet of sail, the Skeeter class is limited to just 75 square feet of sail. Photo credit: Terry Thomas Collection.

Chapter 4

YERKES OBSERVATORY

EYES AROUND THE WORLD TURN TO WILLIAMS BAY

In 1890 the University of Southern California planned to build the world's largest telescope, using glass disks cast by Mantois of Paris and polished into 40-inch lenses by Alvan Clark and Sons, Cambridgeport, Massachusetts. When George Ellery Hale, a younger professor at the University of Chicago, learned the University of Southern California abandoned the project for lack of funding, he urged the University of Chicago to acquire the lenses and construct the telescope and an observatory to house it.

Hale and William Rainey Harper, president of the University of Chicago, approached transit tycoon Charles Tyson Yerkes, who agreed to fund the facility. On December 5, 1892 Charles Yerkes hired Henry Ives Cobb, the architect who designed the buildings on the campus of the University of Chicago, to design his observatory. It was built in the shape of a roman cross, with two smaller domes for additional telescopes at the end of each arm.

Prior to being moved to Williams Bay, the 40 inch telescope mount was exhibited at the 1893 World's Columbian Exposition in Chicago. The World's Columbian Exposition was organized to commemorate the 400th anniversary of Christopher Columbus' arrival in the new world. The great Yerkes telescope mount appeared at the north end of the main aisle in Manufacturing Hall. Improvement in telescopes at the time was thought to have reached its limitations with the thirty-six-inch refracting instrument at the Lick Observatory in California. This prediction was proven false by the construction of the great Yerkes instrument on display at the Columbian Exposition in Chicago. The ability to see further into the vast unknown of space was a monumental breakthrough in its time and Williams Bay, Wisconsin was at its center. George Ellery Hale sought a location close to the University, but beyond the smoke, haze, and city lights of Chicago.

Multiple locations in Illinois were offered to the University and a committee of the Board of Directors visited many of them. John Johnston, a retired Chicago lawyer and real estate speculator who owned acreage on the north shores of Geneva Lake, extended an invitation to the site committee to visit his "gardener's" house in Lake Geneva. Johnston told the committee 'he has a team of horses and will drive them wherever they need to go. He looks forward to showing them the "ideal site" for the new telescope.' December 9th, 1893 Sherburne W. Burnham wrote to Hale, informing him that the Williams Bay site had been chosen and a railroad line already ran from Chicago to Williams Bay, offering easy access. The 53-acre tract of land, about half a mile north of Geneva Lake, was given to the university by Johnston.

After the location was secured from Mr. Johnston, construction began in April 1895 when the first excavations were made. Many skilled artisans came to Williams Bay to build the Observatory, boarding in homes and rooming houses in Williams Bay. Some brought their families and stayed, making Williams Bay their home.

The first astronomical observations with the completed telescope

1893 The 40-inch refractor telescope was displayed at the 1893 Columbian Exposition. The world's largest refracting telescope was displayed from May to October in the Manufacturers and Liberal Arts Building. The signs on the side of the telescope referenced the University of Chicago, the manufacturer of the telescope Warner and Swasey of Cleveland, OH. The telescope was displayed in the north gallery of the Manufacturers and Liberal Arts building without a lens. The telescope was threatened by one of several fires after the fair but it was saved and installed at Yerkes Observatory in 1897. Photo credit: Deborah Dumelle Kristmann Collection.

were made by Hale and his associates in the summer of 1897. The excellent optical qualities of the new telescope were immediately proven when astronomer Edward Emerson Barnard soon discovered a faint third companion to the star Vega, which had gone undetected even by the skilled astronomer Sherburne W. Burnham using the 36-inch Lick telescope.

Attention turned to Williams Bay on October 21, 1897 when a crowd gathered for the official dedication ceremony of the University of Chicago's great Yerkes Observatory. It was a day of speeches, glorifying both the telescope in its Beaux Arts Observatory and the man who made the whole thing possible, Charles Tyson Yerkes. The observatory's namesake delivered an address presenting the observatory to the University of Chicago. Looking out of place in the crowd of robed scholars, a nervous Yerkes spoke briefly about astronomy, its history, and its "uncommercial" nature saying "There is nothing of moneyed value to be gained by the devotee to astronomy, there is nothing that he can sell; consequently the devotee of astronomy has as his only reward the satisfaction which comes to him in the glory of the work which he does and the results which he accomplishes."

Charles Tyson Yerkes (b. 1837 - d. 1905) Yerkes Observatory was named for its major financial contributor. Yerkes was an American financier who also played a major role in developing mass-transit systems for Chicago and London. Charles Yerkes was know as the "street-car millionaire of Chicago who made a gift of the 40 inch refracting telescope and the Observatory that housed it to the University of Chicago. Photo credit: Chicago Tribune.

1913 George Ellery Hale (b. 1868 - d. 1938) Director of Yerkes Observatory from 1897-1905. American Solar astronomer, best known for his discovery of magnetic fields in sunspots, and as the key figure in the planning or construction of several world-leading telescopes: the 40-inch refractor telescope at Yerkes Observatory, 60-inch Hale reflecting telescope at Mount Wilson Observatory, 100-inch Hooker reflecting telescope at Mount Wilson, and the 200-inch Hale reflecting telescope at Palomar Observatory. Photo credit: Wikipedia: George Ellery Hale.

1895 George Ellery Hale's dog Sirius in front of the partially constructed 90-foot dome. Photo credit: Williams Bay Historical Society.

124

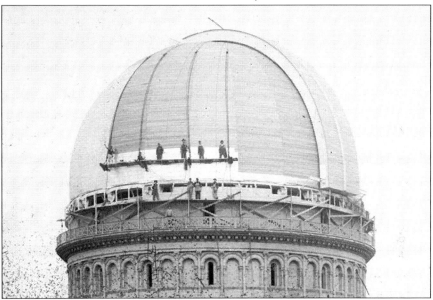

1896 Sheathing and tinning the great dome of Yerkes Observatory October 1896. Photo credit: Astronomy and Astrophysics Journal, Vol. V. No. 5 May 1897.

1896 Construction workers and artisans pose for picture at south entrance to the Observatory. Photo credit: The Astrophysical Journal Vol. V. No. 5, May 1897.

1896 Erecting the iron column for the 40-inch telescope. Photo credit: The Astrophysical Journal Vol. V. No. 5, May 1897.

1896 Erecting the polar axis of the 40-inch telescope. Photo credit: The Astrophysical Journal Vol. V. No. 5, May 1897.

1897 The 40-inch refracting telescope in the 90-foot dome. The telescope tube is 60-feet long and weighs 6 tons. Photo credit: Plate I, The Yerkes Observatory of the University of Chicago, The Astrophysical Journal June 1897.

May 21, 1897 Alvan G. Clark and his assistant Carl Lundin at Yerkes Observatory with the crown lens of the 40-inch refracting telescope. Alvan Graham Clark accompanied the lens to Williams Bay and supervised its mounting only a few days before his death on June 9, 1897. It is interesting to note Alvan Clark had a personal connection to Ashfield, Massachusetts, the hometown of the Israel Williams family. Photo credit: Astronomy and Astrophysics 1897.

1897 Yerkes Observatory power house. Two 8 x 10 Ideal engines each carrying a direct connected Siemens and Halske dynamo with a capacity of 200 amperes at 125 volts powered five electric motors that operated the 40-inch telescope and two larger motors that operated the rising floor and 90-foot dome. Two 14 x 48 tubular boilers supplied steam for heat. Steam pipes for heating, cables for power, and water pipes ran underground from the power house to the Observatory. Mr. E. N. Myers was the engineer in charge of the power plant. Photo Credit: Astronomy and Astrophysics Yerkes Observatory 1897.

1897 Northeast Wing. Photo credit: Plate XIII, The Yerkes Observatory of the University of Chicago, The Astrophysical Journal Vol. VI No. 1 June 1897.

1897 The central rotunda of Yerkes Observatory. Henry Ives Cobb's design for the Observatory is the Romanesque style with somewhat Saracenic details recalling the Church and Monastery of Monreale. The north and south entrances into the rotunda are precisely the same. Photo credit: The Astrophysical Journal June 1897.

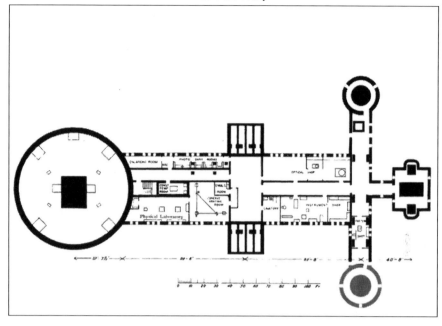

1897 Plans for the observatory. The image above shows the layout of the ground floor and the image below is the main floor. The observatory in the shape of a Latin Cross. Photo credit: Plates X and XI, The Yerkes Observatory of the University of Chicago, The Astrophysical Journal March-June 1897.

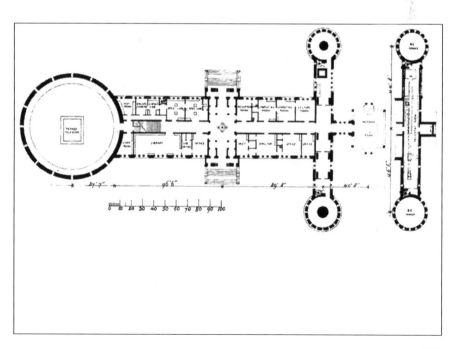

1914 Workers grade the Observatory drive. Facing north toward Geneva Street. Photo credit: Williams Bay Historical Society.

1913 Workers preparing the walk ways on the grounds of Yerkes Observatory. Photo credit: Rick Blakeley.

CONTRUCTION AND COST

When two very perfect glass disks 42-inches in diameter became available George Hale and President Harper of the University of Chicago took an active interest in the establishment of an observatory for astrophysical research. The disks had been cast by Mantois of Paris upon an order from the University of Southern California. Mr. Charles Yerkes agreed to finance the undertaking in September of 1892. Alvan Clark & Sons was contracted to figure the two disks.

Warner and Swasey of Cleveland, Ohio had already built the mounting for the telescope and the 90-foot diameter dome to house it. They also constructed a 75-foot diameter movable floor that raises astronomers to the telescope eyepiece.

Following plans drawn up by George E. Hale Henry Ives Cobb designed the Observatory in a way that combined architectural effect and scientific utility.

The power-house, a part of the original gift from Charles Yerkes, was situated about 750 feet northeast from the center of the large dome. The power-house provided ample electrical current to operate the motors in the shops, for the great dome and rising floor, for the 90-foot dome, and all the general lighting and dark room lamps of the Observatory. Water for all purposes was obtained from the lake by an electric pump at shore operated by electricity from the power-house and stored in a 30,000 gallon tank near the power-house.

The impressive architecture and equipment came with a hefty price tag of $410,000. Edwin B. Frost broke the cost down in "Yerkes Observatory" (1914) as follows:
- Value of land - $30,000
- Refractor lens - $66,000
- Telescope mounting - $55,000
- Dome and rising floor - $45,000
- Remaining cost for building, including the southeast dome and powerhouse and equipment - $150,000
- Kenwood Observatory dome, and equipment - $30,000
- Bruce telescope and building - $9,000
- Snow telescope and building - $10,000
- Grading and planting as of 1914 - $15,000

1914 Looking south toward the Observatory. Workers use mules to grade Yerkes Observatory drive. Baker's barn is shown. Photo credit: University of Chicago Photographic Archive, [apf6-00835] Special Collections Research Center, University of Chicago Library.

October 21, 1897 Dedication of Yerkes Observatory. Those who attended included: Edward Emerson Barnard, A. C. Behr, N. E. Bennett, John A. Brashear, William R. Brooks, Sherburne W. Burnham, Hugh L. Callendar, Henry S. Carhart, E. Colbert, William H. Collins, George C. Comstock, Henry Crew, Susan Jane Cunningham, Charles L. Doolittle, Ferdinand Ellerman, Edmund A. Engler, Albert S. Flint, Edwin Brant Frost, Caroline E. Furness, Father John G. Hagen, S.J., Evelina Conklin Hale, George Ellery Hale, Asaph Hall Jr., William Harkness, William R. Harper, Father John T. Hedrick, S.J., George W. Hough, Margaret L. M. Huggins, William Huggins, George F. Hull, William J. Humphreys, Leslie H. Ingham, George Kathan, James E. Keeler, Kurt Laves, Francis P. Leavenworth, E. E. Lockridge, Henry C. Lord, Carl A. R Lundin, Alva A. Lyon, C. H. McLeod, Malcolm McNeil, Albert A. Michelson, Ephraim Miller, Thomas F. Moran, George C. Mors, Forest R. Moulton, George W. Myers, Simon Newcomb, Ernest F. Nichols, John A. Parkhurst, Henry M. Paul, W. W. Payne, Edward C. Pickering, L. S. Pickering, Mrs. Pickering, Charles Lane Poor, Henry S. Pritchett, Alden W. Quimby, J. K. Rees, George W. Ritchey, C. H. Rockwell, Abbott L. Rotch, Carl Runge, Frederic H. Seares, Mabel Urmy Seares, J. C. Shedd, T. S. Smith, M. B. Snyder, A. G. Stillhamer, Goodwin D. Swezey, Charles B. Thwing, David P. Todd, Milton Updegraff, Winslow Upton, John M. Van Vleck, Frank W. Very, Frank L. O. Wadsworth, Mary W. Whitney, E. J. Wilczynski, Emily Newcomb Wilson, Charles t. Yerkes. Photo credit: Williams Bay Historical Society.

1897 The great dome of Yerkes Observatory open, exposing the great 40-inch refractor telescope to the heavens. Photo Credit: Deborah Dumelle Kristmann Collection.

Circa 1907 View of Yerkes Observatory from the south. Photo credit: Michelle Bie Love.

Circa 1898 Looking east from the northeast tower of Yerkes Observatory: power house, professor's house, and director's house. Geneva Lake is in the background. Photo Credit: Williams Bay Historical Society.

Circa 1897 Home of E. E. Barnard at Yerkes Observatory. Photo credit: Williams Bay Historical Society.

Circa 1917 Edward Emerson Barnard Photo credit: University of Chicago Photographic Archive, apf6-00206, Special Collections Research Center, University of Chicago Library.

1921 Albert Einstein, the staff and faculty of Yerkes Observatory, and other visitors photographed with the 40-inch refractor telescope. When Albert Einstein traveled to the United States in 1921 he said there were only two things he wanted to see: Niagara Falls and Yerkes Observatory. Photo credit: University of Chicago Photographic Archive, apf6-00415, Special Collections Research Center, University of Chicago Library.

Circa 1921 View of Yerkes Observatory from the northeast. Photo credit: Maggie Gage.

1921 Engagement party of Dorothy Block (seat in front of wagon) and Dr. John Paraskevopoulos attended by Yerkes Observatory staff: Mr. Koeppen, Elsie Johnson, Anna Greenleaf Parkhurst, John A. Parkhurst, Florence Baldwin Lee, Edward E. Barnard, Oliver J. Lee, Harriet M. Parsons, Ella Blakslee, Ida Barrett, Esther Searles, Lela D. Cable. Photo credit: Terry Thomas Collection.

Circa 1915 Known as the Director's house, this was the home of George Ellery Hale at Yerkes Observatory, Photo Credit: University of Chicago Photographic Archive, apf6-00690r, Special Collections Research Center, University of Chicago Library.

136

Circa 1934 Brantwood home of Edwin B. Frost on Dartmouth Road. Photo credit: Bay Leaves.

Circa 1930 Edwin Brant Frost. Photo credit: University of Chicago Photographic Archive, apf6-00248, Special Collections Research Center, University of Chicago Library.

Circa 1936 Home of Dr. and Mrs. George Van Biesbroeck. Dr. Van Biesbroeck was one of the world's leading astronomers, a professor at the University of Chicago, and a pillar of the community. He was clerk of the Williams Bay School Board for 21 years and an avid supporter of the Boy Scouts. Mrs. Julia Van Biesbroeck was an accomplished artist and served as president of the Williams Bay School PTA and the Williams Bay Garden Club for seven years. Photo credit: Bay Leaves, Frank Van Epps Editor and University of Chicago Photographic Archive, apf6-01178, Special Collections Research Center, University of Chicago Library.

Circa 1932 The Morava Family of Cedar Point Park tour the exterior balcony of Yerkes Observatory. An extended view of beautiful Geneva Lake and the surrounding countryside could be seen from 44 feet above the ground and 240 feet above Geneva Lake. Photo credit: Morava Family.

Some of the beautiful architectural detail on the exterior of Yerkes Observatory, designed by architect Henry Ives Cobb. Photo credit: Deb Soplanda.

Chapter 5

HOME SWEET HOME

SETTLERS/INFLUENTIAL PEOPLE/ASSOCIATIONS

Whether it was a one-room cabin or a lakefront mansion, the owners proudly called them home. The first home in Williams Bay was built in 1838 by Royal and Israel Williams. By the early 1840s this home would be a stagecoach stop called the Buck-horn Hotel on the route from Southport (later Kenosha) to Beloit.

Williams Bay grew steadily in the last quarter of the nineteenth century. Subdivisions were platted and homes were built. Farms dotted the landscape to the west, north, and east of Williams Bay.

Formally established on May 20, 1854, East Delavan Union Cemetery is the final resting place of many residents of Williams Bay. The first burial at the cemetery was in 1843 following the accidental death of Alexander Utter, who died when the well he was helping to dig caved in on him. Other burials took place at the cemetery between 1843 and 1854 but because of little or no early record keeping it is not known the exact number of early burials which took place. Captain Israel Williams, his wife Lavina, and two of their sons, Moses and Austin, were among the early burials. Captain Williams' grave is located near the corner of Bailey and Theatre Roads.

The Village of Williams Bay as it looked in December, 1897. Photo credit: Terry Thomas Collection.

Williams Homestead

The Williams Homestead was located on Geneva Street just east of the location of Barrett Memorial Library. The original Williams home was a log cabin. Later a frame house was built and was a stage stop called the Buck Horn Tavern on the stagecoach line that ran from Southport (Kenosha) to Beloit. According to a diary left by Royal, additions were added to the home in the early 1860s and the 1870s. The view above shows the east and north sides of the house. The view below is from the 1960s and shows the west and north sides of the house. The Williams barn stood on the corner of Geneva and Williams Streets. The Williams homestead was demolished in the early 1960s and Bay View Motel was built on the site. Photo credits: Barrett Memorial Library.

CERTIFICATE No. 11661

THE UNITED STATES OF AMERICA,

To all to whom these Presents shall come, Greeting:

WHEREAS *Israel Williams Senior, of Walworth County, Wisconsin Territory*

has deposited in the GENERAL LAND OFFICE of the United States, a Certificate of the REGISTER OF THE LAND OFFICE at *Milwaukee* whereby it appears that full payment has been made by the said

Israel Williams Senior according to the provisions of the Act of Congress of the 24th of April, 1820, entitled "An act making further provision for the sale of the Public Lands," for *the North West quarter of the South East quarter of Section one, in Township one North of Range sixteen East, in the District of Lands subject to sale at Milwaukee Wisconsin Territory, containing forty acres.*

according to the official plat of the survey of the said Lands, returned to the General Land Office by the SURVEYOR GENERAL, which said tract has been purchased by the said *Israel Williams Senior*

NOW KNOW YE, That the **United States of America,** in consideration of the Premises, and in conformity with the several acts of Congress, in such case made and provided, HAVE GIVEN AND GRANTED, and by these presents DO GIVE AND GRANT, unto the said *Israel Williams Senior*

and to his heirs, the said tract above described: TO HAVE AND TO HOLD the same, together with all the rights, privileges, immunities, and appurtenances of whatsoever nature belonging, unto the said *Israel Williams Senior* and to his heirs and assigns forever.

In Testimony Whereof, I, *John Tyler* PRESIDENT OF THE UNITED STATES OF AMERICA, have caused these Letters to be made PATENT, and the SEAL of the GENERAL LAND OFFICE to be hereunto affixed.

GIVEN under my hand, at the **CITY OF WASHINGTON,** the *Tenth* day of *September* in the Year of our Lord one thousand eight hundred and *forty four* and of the *INDEPENDENCE OF THE UNITED STATES* the *Sixty ninth*

BY THE PRESIDENT: *J Tyler*
By *J J Tyler jun* Sec'y.
J H Laughlin RECORDER of the General Land Office.
Signed by Recorder 21 Mar 1845

1844 One of many U.S. Land Records recording the sale of land to Israel Williams in southeast Wisconsin. This record describes the land as "North West quarter of the South East quarter of section One in Township One. North of Range sixteen East in the District of Sands subject to sale at Milwaukee Wisconsin Territory, containing forty acres." Dated September 10, 1844. Photo credit: U.S. Land records.

WILLIAMS FAMILY TREE

Ephraim Williams
b. 1747–d. 1839
  m. **Mercy Daniels**
  b. 1757–d. 1793
    Capt. Israel Williams, Senior
      b. 24 Sept 1789 Hampshire County, MA
      d:14 Oct 1846 Williams Bay, Walworth County, WI

JOY FAMILY TREE

Capt. Nehemiah Joy
b. 1757–d. 1830
  m. **Hannah Leach**
  b. about 1765–d. 1838 Williams Bay, Walworth County, WI
    Lavina Joy
      b.17 Aug 1787 Cummington, Hampshire County, MA
      d. 28 June 1852 Williams Bay, Walworth County, WI

FAMILY TREE OF ISRAEL AND LAVINA WILLIAMS

Moses Daniels Williams *(b. 1809–d. 1845)*
  m. Lucinda *(b. ?–d. ?)*
William Williams *(d. 1811 age 1.5 days)*
Israel Williams Junior *(b. 1812–d. 1883)*
  m. Eliza *(b ? - d. ?)*
    (Children of Israel Jr. and Eliza)
      Henry Williams (b. 1837–d. ?)
      Mary Williams (b. 1839–d. ?)
      Milton Williams (b. 1842–d. 1865)
      Almira Williams (b. 1838–d.?)
Rev. Francis Williams *(b. 1814–d. 1896)*
  m. Mahala R. Badger *(b. 1821–d. 1901)*
    (Children of Francis and Mahala)
      Edward F. Williams (b. 1845–d. 1869)
      Charles H. Williams (b. 1848–d. 1874)
      Mary E. Williams (b. 1851–d. ?)
Lavina Williams *(b. 1816–d. 1876)*
  m. John Fowle, Jr. *(b. 1818–d. 1855)*
    (Children of Lavina and John Fowle Jr.)
      Mary Lavina Fowle (b.1841–d. ?)
      Royal J. Fowle January (b.1845–d. 1845)
      Royal A. Fowle (b. 1846–d. 1864)
      Israel W. Fowle (b. 1850–d.1936)
      Harriet Fowle (b. 1854–d.)

Royal Joy Williams *(b. 1818–d. 1886)*
   m. Lucretia Smith Warren *(b. 1824–d. 1907)*
    (Children of Royal and Lucretia)
      Edward F. Williams *(b. 1847–d.?)*
        m. Marie R. Bernhardt *(b 1866–d. 1901)*
        (Children of Edward and Marie)
         June Williams (b. 1891–d. 1897)
         Webster Wanamaker Williams (b. 1892–d.1958)
         Frank E. Williams (b. 1894–d. 1940)
         Helen Dorothy Williams (b. 1899–d.?)
      George Williams *(b. 1848–d. 1924)*
      Ellen Williams (b. 1855–d. 1869)
      Harley Williams (b. 1861–d. 1910)
        m. Matilda Piggins *(b. 1864–d. 1940)*
        <u>(Children of Harley and Matilda)</u>
         Harley R. Williams (b. 1887–d. 1965)
         Ellen (Nattie) Williams (b. 1894–d. 1994
         Lucretia Matilda Williams (b. 1897–d.?)
Austin Jackson Williams (b. 1820–d. 1845)
   m. Elisa ? (b. ?—d. ?)
    (Child of Austin and Elisa)
      Austin Williams (b. ?–d. 1846)
Hannah Leach Williams (b. 1822–d. 1850)
   m. Robert E. Russell (b. 1811–d. 1888)
    (Children of Hannah and Robert)
      Francis William Russell (b. 1839 - d. 1909)
      Robert E. Russell Jr. (b. 1845–d. 1863)
      Lavina A. Russell (b. 1847–d.?)
Fordyce Williams *(b. 1824–d. 1825 age 7 months)*
Fordyce Williams *(b. 1828–d. ?)*
Festus Allen Williams *(b. 1833–d. 1908)*
   m. Albertine Lucy Stevens *(b. 1838–d. 1927)*
    (Children of Festus and Albertine)
      Fordyce Williams (b.1856–d.?)
      Flora W. Williams (b. 1858–d.?)
      Helen W. Williams (b. 1874–d. 1972)
        m. William Chancy Dean *(b. 1868–d. 1942)*

b*. - born* ***d****. - died* ***m****. - married*

Photo credit: Beckwith's History of Walworth County.

Royal Joy Williams
b. 1818 - d. 1886

Royal was the son of Israel Williams, born in Ashfield, MA. Royal arrived in Walworth County in August 1836. While his brothers Israel, Moses, and Austin settled on the south shore of Geneva Lake, Royal claimed land on the north shore of the lake in Section One in Walworth Township. Royal returned east in 1844 and didn't return to Williams Bay until after the death of his mother Lavina Williams in 1852.

Royal was married to Lucretia S. Warren. They had three sons Edward, George, and Harley and one daughter Ellen.

Royal held several government jobs including surveyor and assessor, He died in the Williams homestead and is buried in Walworth Center Cemetery.

George B. Williams
b. 1848 - d. 1924

George was the son of Royal Williams, born in Massachusetts and came to Williams Bay as a boy. George never married and lived in the family homestead until his death in 1924.

George is buried in Walworth Center Cemetery with his parents, brother Harley and sister Ellen. Photo credit: Barrett Memorial Library.

The occasion for this undated photo of George Williams is unknown but the costume appears to have been for an event or parade. Photo credit: Barrett Memorial Library.

Festus Allen Williams
b. 1833 - d. 1908

Festus was the youngest son of Captain Israel Williams. Born in Ashfield, MA, he came to Walworth County with his parents in July 1837. Festus was married to Albertine Lucy Stevens they had three children: Fordyce, Flora, and Helen.

Festus farmed land that is now part of Kishwauketoe Nature Conservancy. Festus is buried in Spring Grove Cemetery in Delavan.

Albertine Lucy Stevens
b. 1838 - d. 1927

Albertine or Lucy, as she was called, was born in Wisconsin, the daughter of Thomas and Armitta (Putter) Stevens.

Albertine is buried alongside her husband in Spring Grove Cemetery.

Photo credit for Festus and Albertine: Walworth County Historical Society.

Helen W. Williams
b. 1874 - d. 1972

Helen was the youngest daughter of Festus Williams. Helen was born in Williams Bay and in 1897 she married William C. Dean, publisher of the newspaper Williams Bay Observer (1896-1897).

Helen and William are buried in Spring Grove Cemetery.

Photo credit: Walworth County Historical Society.

CIVIL WAR SOLDIERS
FROM WILLIAMS BAY AND THE VICINITY

Men, young and old alike, from the area fought in the Union Army in the Civil War. Many returned home to their homes and families but a few died due to disease and injury.

GRANDSONS OF CAPTAIN ISRAEL WILLIAMS

Francis William Russell, (b. 1839 - d. 1909), 9th IOWA Cavalry Co. D.
Robert E. Russell Jr, (b. 1845 - d. 1863), 22nd WIS Infantry Co. D. Paroled from Libby Confederate Prison, Richmond Virginia. Buried in Annapolis National Cemetery, Annapolis, Maryland.
Francis and Robert Russell were the sons of Robert and Hannah Williams Russell, the family lived at Vision Hill above George Williams College.
Royal A. Fowle, (b. 1846 - d. 1864), 1st WIS Heavy Artillery Co. B. Son of John Fowle Jr and Lavina Williams.

BURIED IN EAST DELAVAN UNION CEMETERY

John Charles Kishner, 40th WIS Infantry Co. F.
George Kishner, 49th WIS Infantry Co. K .
John D.C. Gaylord, 28th WIS Infantry Co. K,
Norville Williams, 65th ILL infantry Co. F.
Hugh A. Rector, 10th WIS Infantry Co. A.
Truman Johns, 10th WIS Infantry Co. A.
Oscar F. Vincent, 40th WIS Infantry Co. F.
Henry Southwick, 49th Infantry Co. K.
James Southwick, 49th Infantry Co. K .
Lyman D. Smith, 28th WIS Infantry Co. E,
Russell S. Trumball, 40th WIS Infantry Co. F.
John Spencer, 13th WIS infantry Co. A.
George Farrar, 28th WIS Infantry Co. I.
Clinton Q. Fisk, 9th.WIS Light Artillery.
James Williams, 22nd WIS infantry Co. D.
Robert McChesney, 8th IOWA Cavalry Co. K .

George W. Coburn, Jr. 22nd WIS Infantry Co. D.
Hilas Dalrymple, 49th WI Infantry Co. K .
Hamilton S. Dalrymple, 42nd WIS Infantry Co. F'
William Henry Virgil, 15th IOWA Infantry Co. D.
William L. Bradt, 10th WIS Infantry Co. A.
Henry Dalton, 1st ORE Cavalry Co.
James Snell, 10th WIS Infantry Co. A.
Charles Snell, 10th WIS Infantry Co. A.
Daniel E. Vrooman 49th WIS Infantry Co, K,
George Wilday, 19th WIS Infantry Co. D.
Charles Scoffin, Ensign US Navy.
Otis Dodge, 49th WIS Infantry Co. K.

BURIED IN OTHER IN CEMETERIES.

Sidney Dodge, 4th WIS Cavalry Co. F.
William Dodge, 4th WIS Cavalry Co. F.
Henry DeLap, 49th WIS Infantry Co. K.
John Hall, 2nd WIS Cavalry Co. G.
Charles Remmel, 42nd WIS Infantry Co. F.
Edward B. Meatyard 27th ILL Infantry

Civil War volunteers assembled beneath this Burr Oak in Delavan for muster before boarding trains for Union training camps in Madison and Milwaukee. The historic Muster Tree still stands on the corner of Seventh and Washington Streets and is estimated to be about 270 years old. Photo credit: Deborah Dumelle Kristmann and Michelle Bie Love.

"DOUGHBOYS" FROM WILLIAMS BAY AND THE VICINITY

The United States entered into World War I in April of 1917 when the United States Congress declared war on Germany and Austria-Hungary, an act that joined the armed forces of the United States with those of Great Britain, France, Russia, and Italy to defeat the Central Powers: Germany, Austria-Hungary, the Ottoman Empire, and Bulgaria.

NAME	BRANCH	UNIT	RANK
Ganord A. Andell	Army	44 Bln Serv	Cfr
Donald Kenneth Baker	Navy	USNRF	F 2c
Maynard E. Baker	Army	12 Co 2 AS Mech Regt	Sgt
Warren D. Burdick	Army	Co F 1 Wis Cav	Private
James Drabek	Army	57 Dep Brig	Private
Ivar P. Ericson	Army	161 Dep Brig	Private
Jesse Wilbur Gardner	Navy	USNRF	S 2c
Elmer K. Hansen	Army	Co E 128 Inf	Private 1c
Victor Hansen	Army	Hq 277 Sq AS AS Sig C	Private 1c
Howard Albert Henne	Army	Sec 589 USA Amb Serv	Private
Theodore Roosevelt Johnson	Navy	USNRF	S 2c
Henry J. Kenyon	Army	Btry C 9 TM Btry	Private
James Kochy	Army	Co B 44 Inf	Private
Allen R. Lackey	Army	Hq Det 1 Engrs	Private
Richard John Oetjen	Navy	USNRF	Ch El R
Elmer Pierson	Army	SATC	Private
Axel J. Sandberg	Army	115 Spruce Sq	Private
Oscar Otto Stenstrom	Navy	USNRF	L E R
Joseph Emanuel Wendell	Army	MTC 337	Sgt
Albert Wheeler	Army	156 Dep Brig	Private
Frank Edward Williams*	Army	Co F 64 Inf	Private 1c
Webster Wanamaker Williams*	Army	Q M C	Private
John Atkins	Army	26th Regiment 1st Division	Chaplain
Elmer H. Hopkins	Arny	Regiment 2, company 12.	
Paul Burrill Jenkins	Army	Base Hospital 22, France	Chaplain
Leslie Ellis Sawyer	Army	Unknown	Private 1c

* Great grandsons of Captain Israel Williams

CIVIL WAR PATRIOTS - OTIS DODGE AND SONS

Otis Dodge (b. 1819 - d. 1894), a farmer originally from New York, and his two eldest sons William (b.1840 - d. 1861) and Sidney (b. 1842 - d. 1926) were among the men from the Williams Bay area who served in the Civil War. The sons mustered into Company F, 4th Wisconsin Infantry Regiment in April 1861 (which became the 4th Wisconsin Cavalry Regiment in 1863). William contracted typhoid and died at the Relay House in Relay, MD, after only four months of service. Wisconsin's 4th fought at the Siege of Vicksburg, the Battle of Port Hudson, and the occupation of Baton Rouge. The surrender at Port Hudson gave the Union Army complete control of the Mississippi River and its major tributaries, severing communications and trade between the eastern and western states of the Confederacy. Sidney was wounded at Port Hudson, Louisiana in 1863. He survived the war and was mustered out May 28, 1866.

Otis Dodge and his wife Hannah Sherman had 12 children. According to census records Dodge had moved to Geneva with his family by 1850. Plat maps dated 1873 show Dodge's homestead just northeast of Williams Bay on the north side of what is now Geneva Street across from Cedar Point Park.

Following the war, Sidney became a farmer and moved to Wheeler, Wisconsin, where he died in 1926.

1873 Plat map of Linn Township. Photo credit: Deborah Dumelle Kristmann Collection.

Circa early 1900s Otis Dodge homestead located on the northeast shore of Williams Bay. Photo credit: Tom and Kathy Leith.

1860 A full-length tintype portrait photograph of Otis Dodge who served in the 49th WIS Infantry Co. K. Photo credit: Wisconsin Veterans Museum WVM.1293.I001.

1860 A full-length tintype group portrait photograph of William (left) and Sidney Dodge. Photo credit: Wisconsin Veterans Museum WVM.1293.I002.

Danish Immigrants Christian and Niels Hansen
A Legacy of Contribution and Community

In the mid 1800s, adventurous, hard working entrepreneurial immigrants were drawn to the United States as "a land of opportunity." Brothers Niels and Christian Hansen were among the earliest settlers who came to Williams Bay around 1863 from their native Denmark.

1873 Linn Township Plat Map showing the location of the original Hansen homestead Photo credit: Deborah Dumelle Kristmann Collection.

Christian and Niels were two of seven Hansen children. They were Methodists from Maribo District of Denmark near Copenhagen. Oral family history indicates that the young men came with other families (possibly neighbors Jensen, Madsen) from their native community in Denmark. Christian, the oldest son, was probably motivated by economic problems in Denmark, which was by far the greatest reason why most Danes left for foreign shores. Their intention was to purchase land in Williams Bay speculating to sell it to newcomers and help build a thriving community.

The Hansen family believed strongly in a sense of community and contributed immensely to the prospering village of Williams Bay. They shared the vision of a bustling community as the train and Yerkes Observatory drew new residents and visitors to the area. Owning much of the land between the lake and what is now route 50, 1931 documents for the construction of highway 36 show Victor sold the land to the state which allowed access to the Bay from the northeast.

Christian Hansen (b. 1842 in Denmark - d. 1919) arrived in Walworth, County 1863 or earlier. He was a stone mason by trade and enlisted in the army in 1875. He married Christine (b. 1836 - d. 1905), they had no children.

Niels Peter Hansen (b. 1856 in Den-

mark - d. 1927) was also a stone mason and farmer. He farmed for a living

and was also a caretaker for the Crane estate for 40 years. Niels married Hansine Jorgensen (b. 1857 - d. 1936) They had five children but only three survived into adulthood: Victor (b. 1891 - d.1962), Sadie (b.1893 - d. 1956), and Elmer (b. 1895 - d. 1976).

Victor Hansen Married Elsie Boorman (b. abt. 1893 - d. 1947) in 1921. They had one son, Melvin J. Hansen (b. 1922 - d. 2010).

Victor Hansen served in WWI and was honorably discharged in 1919. Victor earned a living in the Bay by helping his father on the farm and running the family businesses in town:  Hansen's Garage and Livery Service. The Livery transported guests between the Williams Bay train depot, Lake Lawn Lodge and the surrounding area. It was at Lake Lawn Lodge, where Victor met

Elsie Boorman from Merrill, Wisconsin who was a summer employee. After Victor and Elsie married she became a beloved teacher in Williams Bay. Later, while Niels was still living, Victor took over the family businesses. Victor acquired the pier business from Frank Walker and Elmer Hopkins in 1930 through an agreement to settle wages owed to Victor. This occurred during the Great Depression which caused financial hardships for many.

Victor was a founding member of the Volunteer Fire Department and its first Fire Chief. Hansen donated the land for a fire station and led the fundraising efforts to build it. In later years Victor sat as a Village trustee and was a Walworth County supervisor.

Melvin J. Hansen married Lillian C. Ledwell (b. 1926 - d. 2012) in 1963. They had one daughter, Kathryn. Mel ran Hansen's Pier until the 1970s and then moved the family business to the original farmstead on Laurel Street. He worked there until his death in 2010.

Just like his family before him, Mel believed service and community were of the utmost importance. Mel was a long-time member of Williams Bay Volunteer Fire Department and is noted as having been one of the longest serving firefighters in the state of Wisconsin. Mel was also a founding member of the Williams Bay Rescue Squad of which Lillian was also a member.

Original Hansen Homestead 719 Laurel built in 1863 by Christan Hansen who would have been about 22 years old at the time.

Hansen Homestead 628 E. Geneva Street. Built by Christian Hansen in 1872 and sold to Niels Hansen in 1873.

Source and Photo credit: Tom and Kathy Leith. Danish Census Records

DEVELOPMENT OF WILLIAMS BAY

Mrs. Lucretia Williams, widow of Royal Williams, owned much of the land that made up the early Village. In 1883 she sold five acres on the south side of the Williams farm to James Loft and sold another five acres to John Hansen in 1889.

Development in Williams Bay began in earnest with the arrival of the Chicago & North Western railroad in 1888. The original plat of Williams Bay contained Block No. 1 to 6 and Lots 1 to 17 in block 7. The plat was signed by Lucretia Williams and William G. DeGroff. The plat was recorded on July 3, 1889.

The Hansen Addition was platted by Christian Hansen when he subdivided part of his farm east of the Village. The plat was recorded on March 26, 1894.

John Johnston Jr. platted Observatory subdivision in 1895, The platted subdivision was recorded on November 20.

W. H. Francis platted land on Elkhorn Road which was recorded on August 20, 1896.

On October 26, 1904 Assessor's subdivision and the Second Observatory subdivision was recorded by the University of Chicago.

The Bethel block was recorded by R. E. Berntson, Chrystan T. Dyrness, Anna O. Gunderson, Markus Kittleson, Michael Walker, Carl Ivan Wendell, and Gustav A. Young. The acreage was bounded by Cherry, Olive, Williams, and Clover Streets.

The original Lockwood Additions platted by Ulysses Lockwood on August 26, 1905. This addition was later replatted.

George J. Johnson recorded Johnson's Addition on September 19, 1905.

The Williams Third Addition which included Block 19 and Lots 20 to 27 Block 7. The addition was platted by Lucretia Williams, C. S. Douglass, and Harley Williams, guardians, on October 9, 1905.

Bay View subdivision was recorded August 10, 1912 by owner Harvey Hatch. Property sales agents were Shanahan Brothers of Delavan.

Mr. and Mrs. Carl F. Carlson platted Carson's Addition on July 1, 1916. The addition was located in the northwest part of the Village.

This was the Village of Williams Bay when it was incorporated in 1919. The Village contained 1,114 acres of land which was bounded on the south by 19,520 feet of lake shore, by Delavan Road (Theatre Road) on the west, by the Peter Johnson farm on the east, and by the township lines of Delavan and Geneva on the north.

Circa early 1890s Lone Oak was a boarding house in Williams Bay. Workers and artisans working at Yerkes Observatory may have stayed here as well as vacationers who came to Williams Bay. Photo credit: Deborah Dumelle Kristmann Collection.

Circa early 1900s The Snidtker family cottage on Walworth Avenue. Photo credit: Nancy Snidtker Baldwin.

153

1911 Two Queen Anne style homes at 92 and 82 West Geneva Street. Neither home has changed a great deal in the past one hundred years. Photo credit: Deborah Dumelle Kristmann Collection.

Circa 1900 A family poses in front of their Williams Bay home. Photo credit: Williams Bay Historical Society.

154

Circa 1920 Waiting for a ride to church on a Sunday. Photo credit: Deborah Dumelle Kristmann Collection.

Circa 1920s Cottages on the west shore of Williams Bay looking east from Walworth Avenue. Photo credit: Nancy Snidtker Baldwin.

Circa 1930s Home of Elmer 'Hoppi' Hopkins and his mother Sara Hopkins at 104 N. Walworth Avenue across the street from 'Bud' Johnson's Bike Rental on the corner of Cherry Street and Walworth Avenue. Photo credit: Carl Hanley.

1905 The Dyrness Cottage was built by C. T. Dyrness about 1900 for less than $500. It was located on Williams Street second house north of Cherry on the west side. Left to Right: Dena, Hilda (mother), Camilla, Enoch, Christian (sitting in chair), Burt, Arthur (with violin). C.T. was one of the founders of Salem Free Church in Chicago. C. T and Art were founders of Lydia Children's Home. Dena married Gus Johnson's son Alvin in 1926. Alvin was one of the founding members of what is now Calvary Community Church. Photo credit: Curt Carlson.

Circa 1935 The Peterson residence on Elm Street. Michael Tobias Peterson was a partner in the Granzow and Peterson grocery store. Photo credit: Bay Leaves, Aug. 14, 1935, sketch artist J. Hennes.

May 1906 Wedding photo of Michael and Lelia Ackley Peterson, children born to the Petersons were Marion, Gladys, Vivian, Hayden, Loretta, and Ardis. Photo credit: Kristin Rees Hunsaker.

Circa 1915 Albert W. Harris' Spanish style home at Kemah Farm where he bred and raised prized Arabian horses. Albert Harris purchased the farm from Festus Williams in 1902. The Harris home at Kemah Farm sat on a hill on the north side of highway 50 overlooking Geneva Lake and Lake Como. Today, two beige stucco gate posts across from Harris Road are all that remain of the former Harris estate. Albert Harris was so protective of his horses that he left a provision that stipulated that his buried horses must be left in perpetuity in their cemetery on his farm. Photo credit: Book of Lake Geneva.

CONGRESS CLUB

Congress Club, founded in 1876, was established as a social and musical club. The club was formed primarily by young married couples who resided near Congress Street on Chicago's west side. In 1881 members purchased ten acres of wooded land on the western shore of Williams Bay. The first of several buildings was constructed in 1882. The Club's architectural significance rests on the 19th century interpretation of the Queen Anne style as an appropriate summer cottage form.

The first three buildings were constructed and completed by July 1882. The three buildings included the clubhouse in the center of the grounds and cottages for Patrick J. Healy (#2) and George Lyon (#10) founders of Lyon and Healy Music Company. Eventually 10 white cottages were built, five on each side of the Clubhouse, forming a semi-circle facing the lake. Originally the Clubhouse served as a communal dining hall and had six apartments on each side of the reception and dining rooms. Today all of the homes have their own kitchen and the historic Clubhouse is used for joint functions.

Founding and early members of the club include: Harvey T. Weeks, President; Charles N. Post, Secretary; George G. Parker, Treasurer; P. J. Healy, George W. Lyon, Frank L. Eastman, Joseph G. Hall, Junius N. Love, Fred S. James, William H. Harper, Henry C. Gray, I. N. Camp, James W. McDonough, George Griswold, James B. Dutch, Florine S. Young, Scott Jordan, George S. Bullock, and George H. Taylor.

Circa 1890s Congress Club members sitting on the veranda of the Clubhouse. Photo credit: Congress Club - Carol Carlson Swed.

Circa 1896 Some of the house in the semi-circle of homes at Congress Club. Photo credit: Congress Club - Carol Carlson Swed.

Circa 1890s Clubhouse at Congress Club. Photo credit: Congress Club - Carol Carlson Swed.

SUBDIVISIONS ON THE WESTERN SHORE OF THE BAY

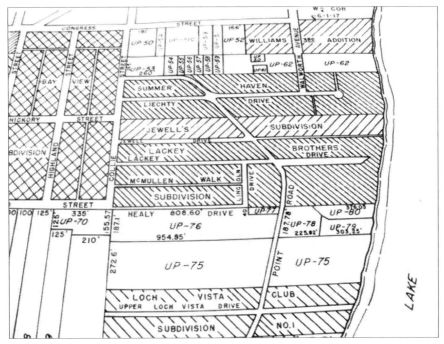

Circa 1920s to 1930s Map of the subdivisions located on or near the western shore of Williams Bay. Photo credit: Phyllis Killar Janda.

The real development of the Village seems to date from the platting of Loch Vista in 1921 by Arthur B. Jensen and Donald F. Abel. The salesmanship of Mr. Jensen called attention to Williams Bay as a summer resort area for people with modest incomes.

Other subdivisions followed, William Lackey and his brother Reuben platted Lackey Brothers subdivision in 1923, Walter Jewell platted Jewell subdivision in 1924, and the platting of Summer Haven by the Wisconsin Transportation Company when the land was purchased from the George Williams estate following Mr. Williams' death in 1924.

Homes built in the subdivision platted by the Lackey Brothers were required to cost no less than $2,000 (circa 1925) and be used as a private dwelling only. Owners were allowed to build one garage for private use, the front of the garage could not extend more than 40 feet from the rear of their property. No other buildings of any type were allowed.

Lackey Brothers subdivision would become known as Oakwood Estates.

LOCH VISTA

Loch Vista subdivision, located on the western shore of Williams Bay, was first conceived by Mrs. and Mrs. Don Abel and Mrs. Abel's brother Arthur Jensen. Pooling their savings, they purchased the upper road property of Loch Vista from Judge William S. Harbert whose home Tre-brah had burned down. The lower road portion was purchased from a family named Bush.

The first meeting of Loch Vista Club members was held on November 21, 1921, at the LaSalle Hotel in Chicago. It was at this meeting that Dr. T. Abel made a motion to organize the club. The Club's constitution stated the purpose of the club was to 'cultivate the social life of the colony and foster improvements of the properties therein.' The Club had a budget of $250 for the 1921-1922 season. The Club decided to retain ownership of the roads. The Club installed a water system and pump house and built a tennis court in 1922-1923. In 1927 the Club purchased lakefront property from J. Hansen for $4,000. In 1929 a pavilion was constructed over the pump house that was large enough to accommodate the afternoon gatherings of the ladies of the club. A gym set was built in 1930.

Original Club members were: A. B. Jensen, D. F. Abel, Dr. T. C. Abel, George Olsen, M. Gunderson, C. Finstad, C. Gunderson, J. Higgins, A. Highland, A. Buland, C. E. Gaul, R. Breckenridge, A. Busch, W. Loomis, N. Nelson, L. Repsold, O. Rosboro, F. Smith, M. Severinghaus, E. Tweed, and I. Viehe-Naese.

Circa 1920s Loch Vista Home. Photo credit: Ruth Karkow.

1916 Upper Road looking toward the lake. Photo credit: Ruth Karkow.

Circa 1930s Club members installed a tennis court in the season of 1922-1923. Photo credit: Ruth Karkow.

OAKWOOD ESTATES

Will Lackey and his brother Reuben platted Oakwood Estates and recorded it as Lackey Bros. Subdivision July 20, 1923.

Circa 1930s Frank Fleishman family home. Photo credit: Phyllis Killar Janda.

Circa 1930s The Fleishman family Oakwood Estates on the pier. Photo credit: Phyllis Killar Janda.

Circa 1930s Row boat ride off of Oakwood Estates. Photo credit: Phyllis Killar Janda.

163

Circa 1930s Henry Ferris home in Oakwood Estates. Photo credit: Phyllis Killar Janda.

JEWEL SUBDIVISION

Walter E, Jewell, a boat builder in Williams Bay, subdivided some of his lakefront property in 1924. Jewell Subdivision was recorded at the Walworth County courthouse on September 23, 1924.

Jewell began building boats in Williams Bay in the late 1880s. Walter Beauvais who had managed Jewell Boat Company for the previous two years purchased the land and buildings from Walter Jewel in 1936. Mr. Beauvais was widely known for the Beau Skeeter ice boat.

SUMMER HAVEN

Lots in Summer Haven subdivision were put up for sale after the land was purchased from the George Williams Estate by the Wisconsin Transportation Company which had used it for storage of its boats for many years.

1935 The residence of Col. and Mrs. John E. Atkins. The Atkins retired from active service in the Salvation Army. During World War I Col. Atkins was a volunteer chaplain with the regiment commanded by Lt. Col. Theodore Roosevelt, Jr. Col. Atkins served as Williams Bay Village President in the 1930s. Photo credit: Bay Leaves, Vol 3 No. 7 June 27, 1935.

CEDAR POINT PARK

Circa 1930s Attractive wood pergola style columns were used throughout Cedar Point Park as street signs. There were similar arched entries on the designated easements leading to all of the parkways. Later the columns were replaced with poured concrete forms and the arched entries to the parkways were removed. Photo credit: Robert Franzen.

Cedar Point Park Association lies along the northeast shoreline of Williams Bay. The point itself is 3/4 of a mile in length, hilly and covered with large oaks and at one time cedars. This area was sacred to the Potawatomi, they called it Ke-she-ge-ki-ah-ke-tah-ke-wun, meaning cedar hill or ridge. To the Potawatomi the cedars represented a deceased spirit, cutting one of these trees meant killing that spirit a second time. The Potawatomi camped everywhere on Cedar Point, but especially on the long sloping parkways leading to the shoreline. After the departure of the Potawatomi in 1836, Cedar Point passed through many hands and remained undeveloped. By the late 1800s, Chicago industrialist, N. K. Fairbank (b. 1829 - d. 1903) owned most of the point. Lakeside estates were built in the later part of the 19th century by Edward B. Meatyard, Herbert A. Beidler, and John M. Smyth. The wooded point became known as Fairbank's Woods and was a favorite camp ground of locals and visitors until the 1920s.

In 1922, Chicagoans Emory F. Jaeger and Alfred A. Pederson purchased the land from the estate of N. K. Fairbank with the intentions of subdividing it. Taking advantage of the natural geography of the land the developer created four beautiful parkways (20 acres and 1800 feet of shoreline) around which each of the proposed 481 lots in the community would share and have easy access to the lakefront, swimming, and piers. By 1925, the Cedar Point Park Association was formed.

Circa 1930s View of Birch Grove (Parkway 4). Franzen residence is on the right. Photo credit: Robert Franzen.

Circa 1930s View of Parkway 5. Decades later, not much has changed on the piers or parkways of Cedar Point Park Association. Likewise, many homes have been passed down from generation to generation. Many neighbors children have grown up together and gotten married and continue to gather on these piers. There must be something very special about this place! Photo credit: The Strandin/Goodlow Families.

Circa 1930s The foundations of the first homes built in Cedar Point Park were dug by horse and plow. Pictured is the beginning of the Morava residence off of Walnut Grove (Parkway 3). Photo credit: Morava Family.

Circa 1920s Oak Grove (Parkway 5), one of eight parkways that residents of Cedar Point Park Association share and enjoy. Resident Calvin Kuder recalls in his recollection of Cedar Point , *Dear Neighbor*, " . . . folks saw one another in the natural course of enjoying summer pursuits." Needless to say, many close friendships have been forged in these parkways and piers over the years. Photo credit: John and Glendia Strandin.

Circa 1930s Access to water was a huge perk to new Cedar Point Park residents. Pump houses were located in four of the main parkways from which lake water was pumped to each home for household purposes. Drinking water was provided by well which proved to be hugely unsatisfactory for many years. Finally in1936, a WPA Federal grant allowed the Village to extend their water service to Cedar Point Park residents. Photo credit: John and Glendia Strandin.

Circa 1930s The Morava brothers; George, Dick, and Bob on the pier of Walnut Grove (Parkway 3). At a time the swimming piers had diving boards. Photo credit; The Morava Family.

Circa 1930s Summer home of Adolph and Martha Helquist family at 194 Circle Parkway. Their son John later became known as John Conrad of Elmer the Elephant fame, a favorite Chicago children's TV show in the 1950s. Photo credit: Keith and Penny Pozulp.

168

Circa early1930s Jonah G. Southwick settled on land a mile or so north of Williams Bay in 1851. Jonah and his wife, Mary Ann, raised their family of twelve children on this farm. William H. Southwick was born on the family farm in 1852 and lived there until his death in 1939. William's son, Ernest continued to farm the land until his son-in-law John Ingersoll took over the farm. Ernest subdivided part of the farm in the 1930s creating Southwick Subdivision. The first owners were from Salem Evangelical Free Church in Chicago. The cottages pictured below were owned by the Hovestol, Sonju, Salverson, and Tonneson families There was a stream with an artesian well, and the man in the foreground is bringing a bucket to the stream to get water. Photo credit Tim Hanson.

This Picture is a view from Elkhorn Road (highway 67) taken a few years later, by then the number of homes, mostly summer cottages, had increased considerably. Renamed Bayview Hills in the 1950s or 1960s, the subdivision is mostly year-round homes today. Photo credit: Bill Anderson.

1895 Tre-Brah was the home of William Soesbe and Elizabeth Boynton Harbert located on the western shore of Williams Bay. William Harbert was an American lawyer, judge, philanthropist, social activist, and Civil War soldier. Some of his activities included serving as president of the Board of Managers for Forward Movement, a social settlement organization; interest in municipal control of public utilities; and establishment of the Juvenile Court and other legal reforms. Elizabeth Boynton Harbert was a suffragist, lecturer, author, and editor. She served on the Board of Managers for the Girl's Industrial School at Evanston, Illinois, and was a social activist. She held leadership roles or was active in such organizations as: Illinois Woman's Suffrage Association, Evanston Woman's Club, and the World's Unity League (formed at the World's Parliament of Religion). Photo credit: Barrett Memorial Library and The Boyton-Harbert Society.

Circa 1902 An Italian Renaissance mansion was erected on the western shore of Williams Bay for a former Methodist Reverend turned "Free Thinking" spiritualist by the name of George Chainey. In 1903, Reverend Chainey formally opened and dedicated his new residence as "Mahanaim." Some of the friends of the movement were neighbors Mrs. Elizabeth Boynton Harbert, Dr. Alice Bunker Stockham, as well as lawyers, doctors, ministers, and members of other religions. Mahanaim Home and School of Interpretation was short lived in Williams Bay when Reverend Chainey moved his school to California. Photo credit: Deborah Dumelle Kristmann Collection.

Circa 1909 Alice Bunker Stockham was born in 1833 in Cardington, Ohio, was an obstetrician and gynecologist, and was the fifth woman to become a doctor in the United States. She specialized in pediatrics and women's reproductive health. In 1897 she launched a New Thought School located in Williams Bay, Wisconsin, known as the Vralia Heights Metaphysical School. A summer school of nature study and philosophy, the school covered topics such as botany, sex, and metaphysics. For eight years Dr. Stockham held conferences at Vralia Heights that were attended by many well-known progressive thinkers of the day. In 1905, Dr. Stockham was charged with sending sexually explicit material through the mail. She was found guilty and fined. Her legal fees prompted the sale of Vralia Heights to Reverend Norman B. Barr and the Olivet Summer Assembly Association in 1909; they renamed it Olivet Camp. The property sold for a total of $9,666.67; $5,666.67 for the property and $4,000 for an encumberance to Wendell Schneider. Photo credits: Norman B. Barr Camp and American Women, 1897.

Circa 1930 Old Bank is a Queen Anne style home built in 1893. Architect William G. Williamson built three homes in this style on Outing Street. The group of three homes was originally known as Wm. G. Williams Subdivision and later Oak Bank. Photo credit: Walworth County Historical Society.

Circa 1880s Lawn Glen, the castellated villa of Edward Brown Meatyard. Edward Meatyard was a civil engineer, holding patents on numerous items used in the railroad industry. He served in the 27th Illinois Infantry in the Civil War earning the rank of Major. Major Meatyard was largely instrumental in bringing the railroad to Williams Bay; he gave the right of way on his land north of highway 50 to the railroad. Photo credit: Picturesque Lake Geneva.

Circa 1880s The view east from Lawn Glen. By 1886 Major Meatyard owned 730 acres of land from the shoreline east of Cedar Point back to Lake Como and most of the flat land at Lake Como as well as 240 acres in the Town of Walworth. Photo credit: Picturesque Lake Geneva.

172

Circa 1920 Alpine Villa, home of Herbert Alpine Beidler. Herbert Beilder purchased Major Meatyard's property in Cedar Point in 1890. Over the years Alpine Villa underwent many alterations and enlargements. Both of the Beidlers were supporters of Lake Geneva Country Club. Mr. Beidler was one of the eleven men present in December 1895 when the club was formed. The Beidlers owned the steam yacht Cygnet. Photo credit: Deborah Dumelle Kristmann Collection.

Circa 1902 Shoreline at Herbert Beidler's Alpine Villa. Photo credit: Michelle Bie Love.

173

TYRAWLEY

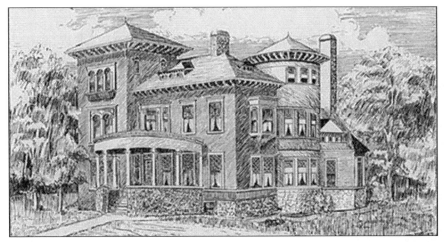

Circa 1896 Tyrawley summer home of the John M. Smyth famiily on the eastern shore of Cedar Point. Photo credit: Chicago Daily Tribune.

Tyrawley, the summer home of John M. Smyth, stood on the eastern shore of Cedar Point at the east limits of Williams Bay. Begun in 1895, the Smyths took possession of the home in the summer of 1896.

The Smyth family spent their first summer on Geneva Lake at Kaye's Park on the south shore directly across from Williams Bay. Two years later, Herbert Beidler sold Mr. Smyth 28 acres and 1100 feet of shoreline, a portion of the land Beidler owned that had been part of Edward Meatyard's estate Lawn Glen, to build his lakeside home Tyrawley.

Circa 1912 John M. Smyth residence and steam yacht Loreto. Photo credit: Deborah Dumelle Kristmann Collection.

Tyrawley had a large carriage house with living quarters for their coachman, a gazebo reaching out over the water, a bath house for family and guests, utility outbuildings, and a greenhouse. Swain Nelson and Sons from Chicago designed the lawns, drives, flowerbeds, and stocked the Smyth's greenhouse.

John M. Smyth died in 1909 from bronchial pneumonia. The Smyth family kept Tyrawley until 1916.

John Smyth Jr. purchased the old Bailey home and land on Geneva Street. The home was remodeled and enlarged and the grounds landscaped. The Smyth family remained there for 33 years.

HEALY ESTATE

Circa 1900 Lakefront home of the P. J. Healy family on the western shore of Williams Bay. Photo credit: Barrett Memorial Library.

George W. Lyon and Patrick J. Healy founded Lyon and Healy in 1864, after they moved from Boston to start a sheet music shop for music publisher Oliver Ditson. Ditson told Lyon and Healy by way of encouragement: "If you have good luck, in ten years time you will do a business of $100,000 per year." The new music firm passed that figure before the end of their first year.

The P. J. Healy family came to Williams Bay as part of the original members of the Congress Club in 1882. The growing Healy family prompted Mr. Healy to purchase several acres of land to the north of Congress Club for the new Healy home.

Unfortunately, Mr. and Mrs. Healy would not spend many summers at their home on the western shore of Williams Bay. Mrs. Frances Healy died in 1899 and Patrick J. Healy in 1905.

In 1919, the eldest Healy son Marquette and his wife Annie purchased land and built their brick home just south of the Healy estate naming it Woods Brook.

The Healy children would remain at the lake for over twenty-five years after their parent's deaths.

Circa 1900 P.J. Healy Family in Williams Bay. Photo credit: Patrick J. Healy, An Appreciation.

Circa 1935 The M. A. Healy home built in 1919 called Woods Brook. When Mr. and Mrs. Niehoff purchased the home they renamed it Towering Elms. It remained a private residence until 2016 when it was demolished. Photo credit: Deborah Dumelle Kristmann Collection.

DRONLEY

Circa 1902 Dronley, summer home of William and Joan Chalmers on the western shore of Williams Bay. Photo credit: Lake Geneva Library.

The William J. Chalmers were very active in the social and philanthropic life on Geneva Lake in the first part of the twentieth century. Their home Dronley near Collie Point was the scene of many of the grandest parties on the lake.

William Chalmers married Joan Pinkerton, the only daughter of Allen Pinkerton, founder of the Pinkerton Detective Agency, on October 21, 1878. William Chalmers was described as a dashing and handsome young man and Joan Pinkerton Chalmers was a striking and charming brunette. Both loved the arts and music.

William Chalmers, who inherited and grew his father's company Fraser & Chalmers, was President of the Commercial Club of Chicago and Director of the Field Museum of Natural History. Fraser & Chalmers merged with Allis Engine Works resulting in the Allis-Chalmers Company producers of farm equipment and mining machinery.

After the death of their children, Thomas Stuart Pinkerton Chalmers and Joan Chalmers Williams, the Chalmers left Geneva Lake and Dronley was sold to Sunday School Association Camp in 1918.

Circa 1900 William J. Chalmers, co-founder of Allis Chalmers Company. Photo credit: Chicago Tribune.

1878 Joan Pinkerton Chalmers on her wedding day, October 21, 1878. Photo credit: Chicago Tribune.

Chapter 6

A PICTURE OF LIFE IN THE BAY

PHOTOGRAPHER GEORGE BLAKSLEE AND OTHERS

George C. Blakslee (b.1861, d.1950) was a noted photographer for George Williams College Camp and Yerkes Observatory in Williams Bay. When the first Congregational Church was destroyed by fire in 1911, he was enlisted by the local Ladies Aid Society to assist in a fundraiser to help rebuild the beloved church. For $1 members of the Ladies Aid Society (and their husbands) would offer to perform a multitude of chores and odd jobs for the Williams Bay community. They washed windows, floors and dishes, beat rugs, cut hair, mended clothing and performed yard work for their friends and neighbors. Blakslee documented these activities in a series he called "A Day in the Bay". Over one hundred years later this extraordinary series of images provides a unique opportunity to see Williams Bay as it was, and its community at work helping each other.

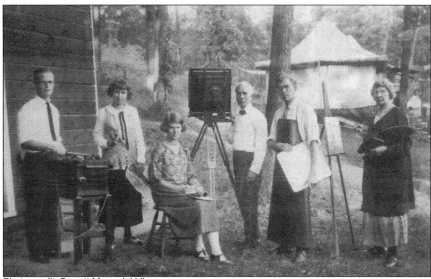

Photo credit: Barrett Memorial Library.

1914 From the 1880s through the 1920s, rugs were taken outside, hung over a line and hit repeatedly with a broom or rug beater. Beating the rug was a good chore for active children or stressed wives and mothers. Photo credit: The United Church of Christ (Congregational) - Williams Bay.

1914 This image taken at 257 W. Geneva St. showing the spring time chore of putting up the screen windows. Photo credit: The United Church of Christ (Congregational) - Williams Bay.

1914 Cleaning windows and hanging storm windows was no easy task! A few tips for clear shiny windows back in the day: use no soap on window glass, instead use old muslin and a clean soft water. A cotton cloth dipped in a little alcohol will add brilliance to the final rub. For added shine dip a rag in paraffin and buff to obtain a brightness impossible to achieve with water alone. Photo credit: The United Church of Christ (Congregational) - Williams Bay.

1914 Two young ladies outside 92 W. Geneva St., probably dressed up and cleaning dishes outside for the picture. Putnam's Household Handbook suggests dishes are washed in hot soapy water and rinsed in clear, cold water—they will not have to be dried. A tablespoon of ammonia can take the place of soap. Photo credit: The United Church of Christ (Congregational) - Williams Bay.

1914 A woman's work is never done. Nice image showing the exterior details that once adorned 92 W. Geneva St. Photo credit: The United Church of Christ (Congregational) - Williams Bay.

1914 A plain wringer was the most common piece of laundry equipment in homes across America in 1900. Soap, starch, and other washing conveniences became more abundant and more varied. Washing once a week on Monday or "washday" was the established norm. Photo credit: The United Church of Christ (Congregational) - Williams Bay.

1914 A young mother taking time out of her busy day to play in the yard with her toddler and dog. Just like today, fresh air and regular naps were part of a healthy routine for a young child. However, over-stimulation such as tickling was strongly discouraged (even criminal), as it was thought to affect the development of the nervous system making the child "fretful and nervous." Photo credit: The United Church of Christ (Congregational) - Williams Bay.

1914 A man carrying a heavy load into the village passing 106 W. Geneva St. on the left. Barrett Memorial Library can be seen down the road to the right. Photo credit: The United Church of Christ (Congregational) - Williams Bay.

1914 Work often required the help of a friend or neighbor. These men are planting bushes maybe for a privacy screen on the property. Photo credit: The United Church of Christ (Congregational) - Williams Bay.

Circa 1920-1933 Car goes of road at bridge in Williams Bay during Prohibition. Ratification of the 18th Amendment to the Constitution banned the manufacture, transportation and sale of intoxicating liquors Photo credit: Terry Thomas Collection.

Circa 1920 Birthday parties were a special event for a child in the 1920s and an occasion to dress in their Sunday best for the party. Wonder who was the birthday girl or boy? Photo credit: Williams Bay School Alumni Association.

1914 Two little boys enjoying ice cream cones on a warm spring day. An ice cream shop was located on or near the location of the 1936 Fire Department Building on Geneva Street. Note the building in the background with the Pillsbury's Best Flour sign which was located near the depot. Photo credit: The United Church of Christ (Congregational) - Williams Bay.

1914 Early image of workers near the lakefront and train depot. This building may have been the location of Douglass & Dunn Flour and Feed which was located in Williams Bay for a short time in 1907. In the background logs cleared from new lots and developments along the lake shore are stacked to the right. Photo credit: The United Church of Christ (Congregational) - Williams Bay.

1914 Maintaining a clean kitchen floor was an involved process. For waterproofing an application of paraffin oil was applied and left to dry. Washing the floor involved a mop dipped in a pail of water with ammonia for extra brightness and shine; candle grease mixed with equal parts of turpentine made for an excellent floor polish. Photo credit: The United Church of Christ (Congregational) - Williams Bay.

1914 Housewives' days were planned: wash on Monday, mend on Tuesday, iron on Wednesday, churn on Thursday, clean on Friday, bake on Saturday, and rest on Sunday. Following this routine ensured butter and bread would be freshly made for Sunday and the house was clean for guests. Photo credit: The United Church of Christ (Congregational) - Williams Bay.

1914 Putnam's Household Handbook of 1916 suggested getting the day's work done in the morning. That way the afternoon was free for sewing, visiting neighbors and friends, receiving company, or simply resting. Photo credit: The United Church of Christ (Congregational) - Williams Bay.

Circa 1900 William Peter Snidtker, an early resident of Williams Bay, was a chauffeur for Richard Teller Crane owner of the Geneva Lake estate Jerseyhurst and founder of Crane Company manufacturer of valves and fittings. W. P., as he was called by family and friends, was married to Gena Dell Snidtker and father of long-time Williams Bay residents Dick Snidtker and Grace Snidtker Ladd. Photo credit: Nancy Snidtker Baldwin.

Circa 1917: Williams Bay resident and businessman, Elmer Hopkins was a veteran of World War I. Photo credit: Carl Hanley.

Circa 1925 Playing outdoors on warm summer days kept children happy and active. Photo credit: Grandpa's Big Book-Carol Stenstrom Ortiz.

Circa 1930s A little girl hugs her doll and Teddy bear at the family cottage in Cedar Point. Photo Credit: John and Glendia Strandin.

Circa 1925 Little boy riding his Irish Mail Car on the sidewalk by his home. Photo credit: Grandpa's Big Book-Carol Stenstrom Ortiz.

A PICTURE OF LIFE ON THE FARM

In the early years of the village, Williams Bay was a rural community with farms to the north, east, and west and cows and horses were even kept in the village. As late as the early 1900s the descendants of Israel Williams still sold milk from the cows on their original plot of land in the Village.

1914 Farmers driving teams of horses pulling wagons was a common sight on the roads coming into the village. Farmers sold or traded eggs and produce at the local general store. Typically farmers only came into the village to purchase supplies only once or twice a month. Photo credit: The United Church of Christ (Congregational) - Williams Bay.

1914 A man with his dog Yerkes Observatory is in the background. Photo credit: The United Church of Christ (Congregational) - Williams Bay.

1914 Cooking and cleaning required water to be carried into the house from the hand pump in the yard. Photo credit: The United Church of Christ (Congregational) - Williams Bay.

1914 Farming was hard work and days started at sunrise and often didn't end until sunset. Photo credit: The United Church of Christ (Congregational) - Williams Bay.

Circa 1920s Farm family with their new automobile. Photo credit: Nancy Snidtker Baldwin.

1914 Portrait of a young farm family. Photo credit: The United Church of Christ (Congregational) - Williams Bay.

1914 Farm wife brings in the eggs from the hen house. Often eggs were sold or exchanged for goods at the general store. Photo credit: The United Church of Christ (Congregational) - Williams Bay.

1914 Young and old alike worked on the family farm. Huldah Wilkins Stam (1852-1938) carries buckets of milk to the house. Huldah was the wife of Charles Stam. Photo credit: The United Church of Christ (Congregational) - Williams Bay.

1914 A little girl plays in a nest of hay her Daddy has raked. Photo credit: The United Church of Christ (Congregational) - Williams Bay.

1914 Grandma and grandson take a break to pet the family cat. Farmer kept cats in the barn to catch mice and other vermin. Photo credit: The United Church of Christ (Congregational) - Williams Bay.

1914 A young couple pose on the porch of their home. Is the reflection in the window East Delavan Baptist Church or the Latter Day Saints Church? Photo credit: The United Church of Christ (Congregational) - Williams Bay.

Circa 1930s Southwick's farm on Elkhorn Road. This farm was settled in 1849 by Jonas G. Southwick; Jonas died here in 1894. His son William Harrison Southwick was born on the farm in 1852 and also died there in 1939. The farm was later owned by Ernest Southwick, son of William, and later by Ernest's daughter and son-in-law Mary and John Ingersoll. In the background is the home and greenhouse that was owned by William and Louise Wolfer. Photo credit: Tim Hanson.

1914 Prosperous families in the Village had domestic help for chores. Here the lady of the house and her maid are taking a break from spring cleaning chores. Photo credit: The United Church of Christ (Congregational) - Williams Bay.

1914 Mrs. Alfred Lindquist making cheese. Mrs. Lavina Williams, wife of Captain Israel Williams, was the first person known to have made cheese in Walworth County. Mrs. Williams made 800 pounds of cheese in one year. Photo credit: The United Church of Christ (Congregational) - Williams Bay.

1914 Mrs. Carrie Davis taking down the wash on a windy day. The Davis family lived on a farm just west of Williams Bay. Note the farm buildings in the background. Photo credit: United Church of Christ-Williams Bay.

1914 Women often milked the cows, cared for pigs and poultry, tended the kitchen garden, and did all the housework too, working from sunrise until sunset. Photo credit: The United Church of Christ (Congregational) - Williams Bay.

Circa 1900s This horse-drawn sickle hay mower was pulled by two horses. The long arm with teeth did the cutting. The mower cut the hay just inches above the ground and the hay fell in a thin layer on the ground where it was left to dry. Development of horse-drawn hay mowers and reapers by Cyrus McCormick and others revolutionized agriculture production in the mid-1800s. Photo credit: Nancy Snidtker Baldwin.

Chapter 7

PILLARS OF THE COMMUNITY
CHURCHES/SCHOOLS/ORGANIZATIONS

As pioneers and settlers came to Williams Bay, they brought much more than their belongings; some brought their extended families and their friends, they brought their traditions and customs, and their religious beliefs.

Motivated by opportunity, those who came were no doubt interested in building a new place to call home. It could be said that the foundation of a thriving community can be found in the churches, schools, and the many organizations that support it. The churches in the Village of Williams Bay provided the community places to gather, educate, worship God, and serve the community.

Many other independent and nationally recognized organizations were formed as well, some groups were formed centering around similar interests (gardening), or for specific community service actions, as well as education and building good moral character (Boy Scouts and Girl Scouts).

Mens and womens groups organized to support and raise funds for community projects, educate its members on current events, fine arts and culture, and world political and social issues.

These groups supported the building and growth of the Village, churches, and school, working tirelessly to beautify the Village and raise money for specific community projects.

CHURCHES

Church was an important part of the lives of residents in Williams Bay. The first organized church in the Village was the Free Evangelical Lutheran Church on the southwest corner of Geneva and Williams Streets, formed in 1891. Many of the early Bay residents had a strong Scandinavian heritage and because of this, services in Swedish and Norwegian were alternated weekly. For this reason the church became known as the Scandinavian Church.

A small church west of the village on North Walworth Road, near the intersection with highway 67 and County Road F, served residents who wanted services in English. In November of 1895, this group of Williams Bay residents arranged to hold services on Sunday afternoon at the Scandinavian Church led by Rev. M. N. Clark from the Walworth Congregational Church. This move may have been made for convenience. Since the decision was made in November, it may have been due to the difficulty of winter travel.

Only a month later a Ladies Aid Society was formed. One year later in December 1896 the congregation voted to build their own church, purchasing a lot on the northwest corner of Geneva and Valley Streets from Mrs. Lucretia Williams, widow of Royal Williams. The new Congregational Church building was dedicated in August of 1901.

The Free Evangelical Lutheran Church or Scandinavian Church was reorganized in 1921 as the Free Mission Church lead by Michael T. Peterson. The building was enlarged and dedicated in July 1921. In 1922 the name of the church was changed to Gospel Tabernacle.

East Delavan Baptist Church was the first church in our area. It was formed on February 14, 1845, with Reverend Henry Topping being the first pastor and 17 charter members. The congregation first met in the log school house at East Delavan and erected the first church building in 1846.

Another early church was formed in 1885 at the home of Anthony Delap at DeLap's Corner (the corner of Highways 67 and 50). The building was built in 1888 by members of the Reorganized Church of Jesus of the Latter-Day Saints on land donated by member Henry Southwick. The humble little white church with a modest tablet above the door that read: L.D.S. and a belfry with a bell that called members to worship sat at the edge of Southwick's farm on the top of the hill north of Williams Bay.

Circa 1890s East Delavan Baptist Church. Photo credit: East Delavan Baptist Church.

Circa 1900s Latter Day Saints Church. The congregation formed at the home of Albert DeLap in 1885. Charles Burr, a member of the church, was the architect and supervised the construction while the group of 40 members gave liberally of their means and time for its building. The church prospered and baptized many members, the first to be received being Mrs. Emma C. DeLap. By the mid 1920s church membership had dwindled to just a few and the church was closed. Photo credit: DeLap Family.

Circa 1899 In 1891, A. H. Arneson, Eric Anderson, and G. L. Jensen incorporated the Scandinavian Free Lutheran church, bought a lot, and erected a church building. In 1899 the school board arranged to rent the basement of the church for the first school in Williams Bay until the new school building was completed. Photo credit: Deborah Dumelle Kristmann Collection.

Circa 1939 Gospel Tabernacle Church. Photo credit: Calvary Community Church.

Circa 1930s Men of the Gospel Tabernacle Church L to R: unknown, Charlie Anderson, Walter Frey, Walter Kullberg, Carl Anderson, John Ingersoll, Alvin Johnson, Ernest Southwick, Helmer Johnson. Photo credit Tim Hanson.

Circa 1905 The Williams Bay Congregational Church built in 1900 was located on the corner of Geneva and Valley Streets. The church burned on December 3, 1911, probably as the result of a furnace malfunction. Photo credit: Barrett Memorial Library.

Circa 1915 The rebuilt Williams Bay Congregational Church built in 1912 was located at the same location as the church that burned the year before. This church also burned in 1953. Photo credit: Barrett Memorial Library.

1919 Congregation Church Boys Bible class. Photo credit: Williams Bay School Alumni Association.

1925 Congregation Church Boys Bible class. Photo credit: Williams Bay School Alumni Association.

Beginner Sunday School Class of 1921: Ruth Ellen Ohl, Buddie Johnson, Louis Bufford, Francis Bufford, Grace Ella Snidtker, Richard Snidtker, Virginia ?, Carl ?, Eddie Baker, Mildred Baker, Michelin Van Biesbroeck, Percilla Lackey, and Maxene Hoffman. Photo credit: Nancy Snidtker Baldwin.

EDUCATION

The very first school in Williams Bay was organized in November 1899 when State Superintendent of Schools D. D. Harvey met with Village residents at the home of Festus Williams. Arrangements were made to hold classes in the basement of the Scandinavian Church for $5 per month until a permanent location could be built. Funds were appropriated for building a schoolhouse and for erecting a 7x12 foot outhouse on the church property with the stipulation that it would later be moved to the new school yard. A site for the new school was found on the northeast corner of Congress & Collie Streets.

William H. Orme was hired as the first teacher with a monthly salary of $30. When Mr. Orme resigned a couple of months later, Fred Webster, son of Joseph P. Webster of Elkhorn, famous composer of "In the Sweet By and By," was hired for the same monthly salary in January 1900. The first elected school board members were Director: Festus Williams, Treasurer: W.G. De Groff, Clerk: Ferdinand Ellerman.

When the new two-story frame schoolhouse opened in September of 1900, the school superintendent's salary was raised to $50 a month and a second teacher was hired for $30 a month. When the janitor resigned, the school board asked the superintendent to take over the janitorial duties for an additional $6 per month.

But this wasn't the first school associated with the settlers of Williams Bay Moses Williams' wife Lucinda taught the first area school in 1839 at Nine Oaks on the south side of the lake. Her pupils were Festus Williams, three of James Van Slyke's children, two of Squire Bell's children, two of Doctor Woods children, and two of Mr.

Clark's. The Woods and Clark families were recent settlers on the south shore of the lake. Mrs. Williams taught school at the Van Slyke residence in 1840 and at the Robert Russell home at the head of the lake for two terms.

Later one-room school houses were located to the north, west, and east of the village. To the north, just east of Delap's Corner was Vincent School taught by Elizabeth Vincent. Vincent School was located on a farm owned by Jarvis Vincent. A school was located east of Williams Bay in an area that was known as the Irish Woods. The original frame structure known as Woods School was built in 1858. Bay Hill School to the west was the first schoolhouse in District #10 in Walworth Township. Built in 1847, the school was at the southeast corner of the Amos D. Johns farm (the current junction of Highway 67 and County Road F). The school was a frame building that measured 16 x 18 feet and was valued at $100. The school was moved a half-mile east on the north side of the road. In 1930 a new building was erected at this location. One more school in the area was Bailey School near the corner of Bailey Road and County Road F.

In 1915, Vincent School located east of DeLap's Corner voted to join Joint District No. 1. The same year, the School Board, through the efforts of board member Storrs B. Barrett, recognized the need for a high school. With a total cost of $125,000; $108,000 for the site and building and $17,000 for equipment; a new brick school on the southwest corner of Congress and Collie Streets opened in the fall of 1916.

1899 The first school was held in the basement of this church for $5 per month rent. The first teacher was William H. Orme who was paid $30 per month. This was a temporary location until the new two-story frame school was built. Photo credit: Deborah Dumelle Kristmann Collection.

1900 Williams Bay Public School a two-story frame structure on the northwest corner of Collie and Congress Streets. Photo credit: Terry Thomas Collection.

1906 Seventh and eighth grade classes at Williams Bay Public School. Photo credit: Williams Bay School Alumni Association.

1912 Students at Williams Bay Public School. Photo credit: Williams Bay School Alumni Association.

1915 Construction of the new school in Williams Bay. Photo credit: Grandpa's Big Book-Carol Stenstrom Ortiz.

1915 Construction of the new Williams Bay school. Photo credit: Grandpa's Big Book-Carol Stenstrom Ortiz.

1915 The new school on the corner of Congress and Collie Streets opened in September of 1915. Total construction cost was $125,000; $108,000 for the site and building and $17,000 for equipment the new school. Photo credit: Deborah Dumelle Kristmann Collection.

Winter 1915-1916 A view of the new school on a cold winter morning. In 1915 the Village had many open fields and lots. Photo credit: Grandpa's Big Book-Carol Stenstrom Ortiz.

1917 May-pole dance in the old basement gymnasium at Williams Bay School. Photo by George Blakslee. Photo credit: Williams Bay School Alumni Association.

Circa 1915 Early high school domestic science classes were intended to ready young women for their duties in the home in healthy environments and focused on training women to be more efficient household managers. Photo credit: Williams Bay School Alumni Association.

203

Circa 1915 High school shop classes taught boys the basics of home repair, manual craftsmanship, and machine safety. Students learned to use tools to build tables and other wood working projects. Photo credit: Williams Bay School Alumni Association.

1924 Williams Bay School Band. Front row L to R: Dave Ekdahl, ? Budash, Kenneth Chapin, Russel Miller, Marion Proctor, Ray Nicholson, ? Peterson, Ray ?. Middle row L to R: Fred Proctor, Don Weyrauch, Alice Proctor, ? Palm, Marion Peterson, Roy Johnson, Myron Piehl. Back row L. to R: Fred Weyrauch, Vivian Peterson, George Proctor, Mr. Wright, C.R. Otto, Roy Tulane, Wib Johnson. Photo credit: Catsy and Julie Johnson.

1920 First and Second Grade students at Williams Bay School. Photo credit: Williams Bay School Alumni Association.

204

1920 Fifth and Sixth Grade students at Williams Bay School. Photo credit: Williams Bay School Alumni Association.

The old two-story school burned down on the evening of **Friday, September 29, 1922**. Most of the men in town carried water to fight the fire. The fire occurred the year before the formation of the Williams Bay Volunteer Fire Department. George Blakslee photo. Photo credit: Williams Bay School Alumni Association.

1919 The Will Be's basketball team. George Blakslee photo. Photo credit: Williams Bay School Alumni Association.

1920 Williams Bay girls basketball. Skirts and sailor-style blouses were the uniform of the day. George Blakslee photo. Photo credit: Williams Bay School Alumni Association.

Circa 1930s Early Williams Bay high school football team. Photo credit: Williams Bay School Alumni Association.

ONE ROOM COUNTRY SCHOOL

Circa 1890 The first school at East Delavan was built of logs in 1845. I was replaced by this frame building in 1870. Both schools were built on land that was donated by Chancey Woodford, a blacksmith in East Delavan. Mr. Woodford also donated the land for East Delavan Baptist church. Photo credit: East Delavan Baptist Church.

Circa 1900s Another early school in the area was located east of Williams Bay in an area that was known as the Irish Woods. The original frame structure known as Woods School was built in 1858. Photo credit: Woods School.

1912-1913 One more one-room schoolhouse in the area was Bailey School. Ethel Haegeman was the teacher. Located near the corner of Bailey Road and County Road F the one room school was later replaced by a brick structure. This brick building is now houses the Delavan Lake Sanitary District. Photo credit Walworth County Historical Society.

Built in 1930 the Bay Hill School house still stands along highway 67 west of the Village of Williams Bay; today it is privately owned. Photo credit: Michelle Bie Love.

Circa 1930 Interior view of Bay Hill School. Photo credit: Walworth County Historical Society.

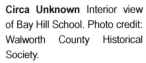

Circa Unknown Interior view of Bay Hill School. Photo credit: Walworth County Historical Society.

207

WILLIAMS BAY MEN'S CLUB

The Williams Bay Men's Club was a civic organization similar to the Lions Club, Rotary Club, Kiwanis Club, and community Chambers of Commerce.

The Club met once a month for dinner at one of the hotels or restaurants in the Village followed by a business meeting to discuss measures for the good of the community.

The Club took the lead in promoting the Village through various means. It had a committee to which solicitation for advertisements were referred, it promoted the Williams Bay Village Sports Day and winter sports. For a number of years it sponsored the All Village Picnic that was held every June.

All men in the Village were eligible for membership and it included many father/son members who joined together. Their meetings often included speakers who spoke about their work or interests.

During its years of service men who served as president of the Club include: William Elbert, Chauncey Grimm, F. Arthur Anderson, Carl M. Bjorge, W. H. Freytag, Dr. Clifford Wiswell, Myron Piehl, and Lawrence Hollister.

WILLIAMS BAY WOMEN'S CLUB

The Williams Bay Women's Club began in 1926 when a group of friends gathered at the home of Hazel Bjorge. The women began discussing all of the activities their husbands were involved in and decided that they too deserved "special evening with friends" and so the planning for the first Women's Banquet began.

May 27, 1934 Luncheon Back Row: Elsie Hansen, Bea Wiswell, Ole Burton, Virginia Rietz, Bee Johnson, Sue Elbert, Esther Hotton, Marge Hotton, Mrs. Doty, Bernice Thompson, Dorothy Gates. Front Row: Ella Mc Connell, Helen Bradt, Hilda Hollister, Marian Freytag, Marion Chamberlain, Miss Schaeffer.

The first banquet was held in the spring of 1927 at Rose Lane Lodge. Tickets for the event were $1 for dinner, entertainment, and a speaker. One hundred and one women attended the first banquet. Entertainment at the first banquet was provided by Mrs. Carl Ridell and Mrs. Theo Johnson who provided violin and vocal solos. The speakers for the evening was Mrs. Ebba Beckus from Beloit who was the principle of a girls school in China and Mrs. John Blodgett of Lake Geneva, the Wisconsin State officer for the National Women's Club. Attendees were asked for a ten cent donation for the purchase of a White Elm tree to be planted in Edgewater Park.

The evening was a huge success and the women voted to make the dinner an annual event. The banquet has been held every year since except during World War II when the banquet was canceled in 1943-1945.

WILLIAMS BAY GARDEN CLUB

The Williams Bay Garden Club began in 1930 at the Women's Banquet. The organization would promote beautification of the Village, increase interest in home gardens, and develop a love of nature for members. Membership fees were $1 a year and club meetings were held on the first Tuesday of the month.

The Garden Club was active in beautifying the Village. They did plantings at Barrett Memorial Library and Edgewater Park. The Club was responsible for the landscaping of the grounds at the Water Works building. In addition the Club planted many of the elm trees and evergreens that lined the streets in the Village and in Edgewater Park.

The Club also presented prizes to Village residents for the most artistic outdoor decorations at Christmas time.

In 1933, the Garden Club of Williams Bay chose the hollyhock as the village flower. The Heavenly Blue morning glory was the second choice. Village residents were urged to "plant many of these flowers."

Presidents of the Williams Bay Garden Club included: Mrs. L. A. Hollister, Mrs. J. J. Hotton, Mrs. G. Van Biesbroeck, and Mrs. W. D. Beauvais. Charter Members: Marion D. Chamberlain, Hilda B. Hollister, Margaret Hotton, Ann Anderson, Berniece Thompson, Marion Freytag, Sue M. Elbert, Elsie Hansen, Esther H. Hotton, and Helen H. Bradt.

TUESDAY NIGHT STUDY CLUB

The social life of the village centered around churches: the Congregational, and Swedish, later called the Gospel Tabernacle, and still later Calvary Community Church.

The Tuesday Evening Study Club was the first Women's organization in the Bay. It was originally known as the Cross and Crescent Society of the Congregational Church originally but began accepting married women in 1929.

The Cross and Crescent Society was formed in the early 1900s by Reverend E. L. Morse, pastor of the Congregational Church. The organization made up of high-school girls, began its studies with Samuel Zwerner's book "The Moslem World." For a number of years studies centered on missionary history and activities such as presenting plays. Funds raised by the Society were used to purchase gifts for the church.

The now grown young women from the Cross and Crescent Society who were still active and interested in studies formed the Tuesday Evening Study Club. Topics covered all types of interests including art, economics, science, and politics. Membership was limited to 25 women due to space constraints in members' homes where meetings were held.

WILLIAMS BAY BOY SCOUTS

On April 30, 1927 the Williams Bay Boy Scouts submitted an application for a new troop charter. Lawrence A. Hollister, F. W. Weyhrauch, and A. C. Ohls were the Scout Committee and the troop was sponsored by the Williams Bay

Public School. The first Scoutmaster was A. C. Carlson and David Erkdahl was the Assistant Scoutmaster. Eleven boys ages 12-15 were enrolled in the troop. In1938 the roster included 29 boys.

The Williams Bay Cub Pack was formed on February 19, 1933. Cubmaster was W. W. Morgan and Assistant Cubmasters were Wilbur Johnson and Volmer Sorenson. The roster included fourteen boys ages 9-11.

The plans to find a permanent location for the Boy Scouts to meet began in the spring of 1932. A tract of land east of the train depot was secured with the help of Charles French, an attorney for the Chicago & North Western Railroad. A five-year lease was signed in June 1932.

The seventeen acre location had rolling hills, was heavily timbered, and contained many forms of plant life, many of which had not been found anywhere else in the area for quite some time.

Circa 1930s Dr. George Van Biesbroeck was instrumental in the building of the Boy Scout Cabin. Photo credit: Barrett memorial Library.

Through the hard work and determination of Dr. George Van Biesbroeck, a staunch supporter of the Williams Bay Boy Scouts, a log cabin was built in an oak grove providing a meeting place and shelter for the scouts.

WILLIAMS BAY GIRL SCOUTS

In the midst of the Progressive Era, and as the nation was expanding by adding the states of New Mexico and Arizona—but before women had the right to vote—Juliette Gordon Low founded Girl Scouts in 1912, with an emphasis on inclusiveness, the outdoors, self-reliance, and service.

From the first gathering of a small troop of 18 culturally and ethnically diverse girls, the Girl Scout Movement was born.

Little is known about the first Girl Scout troop in Williams Bay that was organized in the 1930s.

We do know the first leaders of the troop were Miss Mary Calvert, Mrs. Helen Morgan, and Agnes Drabek.

Chapter 8

VACATION GETAWAY
RESORTS/HOTELS/BOARDING HOUSES

The charming little village of Williams Bay, is situated in a rolling fertile county whose natural beauty has been carefully preserved and enhanced by wise community guidance. An easy three-hour drive or train ride from Chicago brings the traveler to this delightful and interesting spot where simplicity, beauty, and truth are the order of the day, where music, art, and letters, as well as the world of science, have their representation on the shores of America's beautiful Geneva Lake.

And so the Chamber of Commerce of Williams Bay, known by its more modest name of the Men's Community Club, speaks of the dozen places of rest and refreshment with hearty enthusiasm and with assurance that no apologies will be necessary.

RESORTS, INNS, HOTELS, AND BOARDING HOUSES

The Bay Shore Inn - Mrs. Bess Vandercook, proprietor
The Normandie - J. Noble, proprietor
Ferndale Inn - E. R. G Jones; P. G. Nuernberger; Edith Hatch, proprietors
Fernwood and Twin Cottages - Eric Anderson, proprietor
The Clarendell - Mr. and Mrs. Carl Ridell, proprietors
Rose Lane Lodge - J. Jorgensen, proprietor
Sherwood Resort - S. and L. Lundberg, proprietors
Solid Comfort Resort - John Andell, proprietor
Norway Camp - H. Boudorf, proprietor
Maple Grove Resort - A Kaukol, proprietor
Glaudier's Resort - G. Glaudier, proprietor
The Belmont - Mr. Zabrdal, proprietor

Twin Oaks Rooms - Mrs. Zebulon Sawyer, proprietor
Rest Cottage Resort - Mrs. Charles J. Jensen, proprietor
Lake Lane Farm - Mr. and Mrs. Gus Johnson. proprietors
Fine Summer Cottages - Charles Madison, proprietor

Total occupancy at the resorts was approximately 337.

RESTAURANTS AND TEA ROOMS

Homway Restaurant - Mr. Clifton Mustin, proprietor
Mrs. Brown's Tea Room - Mrs. Brown proprietor
Lake View Restaurant -
Mrs. Pearson's Tea Room - Mrs. Pearson, proprietor
Lee's Kitchen - Lela Cable Hopkins
Spence's Dining Room and Bar - Melvyn C. Spence

The scenic beauty of Williams Bay is unsurpassed. There was an 18-hole golf course within the Village with an attractive club house at the service of players without extra charge. Normal daily playing rates prevailed.

Abundant provision is made for swimming, sailing, canoeing, and a complete round of water sports. There is no better fishing anywhere. Blue gill, perch, black bass, and pickerel are the main catch.

Williams Bay is home to Yerkes Observatory of the University of Chicago, where A Century of Progress began.

It is not possible to talk about the resorts that once graced the shores of Geneva Lake without mentioning the famous Whiting House, Pishcotaqua Hotel, and Kaye's Park. The Whiting House was built in 1873 and by 1882 its capacity of 200 guests was taxed. Pishcotaqua Hotel was a four-story hotel with verandas on all four floors. Built in 1881, the Pishcotqua Hotel was 174 feet long and burned in 1892. Kaye's Park, on the south shore of Geneva Lake, was founded by Arthur Kaye in 1873. The park featured a race track, museum, and other attractions that drew early Chicagoans to the Lake Geneva area.

BAY SHORE INN

Circa 1920s Originally a dance hall on Walworth Avenue, the building was moved to the lake front when the dance hall didn't catch on and renamed Bay Shore Inn. The new inn offered guests American and European plan vacations, moderate rates, modern hotel, cottages, dining porch overlooking the lake, home cooked meals, coffee shop, rock pool, flag stone porch with an awning, and summer sports including a large lawn for games or sunning, bathing, large private sand beach, pier, row boats, and fishing. Mrs. Bess Vandercook was manager of the Inn. In 1939, Mr. Le Roy Dearth, of De Kalb, Illinois, leased the Bay Shore Hotel for the summer.

Photo credits: Deborah Dumelle Kristmann Collection.

SOLID COMFORT RESORT

Circa 1920s John and Hannah Andell opened the Solid Comfort Resort on Cherry Street in the early 1920s. The picture of Solid Comfort Resort above is from a postcard that was postmarked in Williams Bay in 1922. A Solid Comfort Resort advertisement from 1924 boasts the resort is larger and better than ever with a new modern annex. The kitchen/ hotel is shown below and the original portion of Solid Comfort above is visible in the far background of the picture to the right. The photos to the right and below are of Solid Comfort Resort in the 1930s.

Photo credits: Keith Otzen and Deborah Dumelle Kristmann Collection.

FERNWOOD AND TWIN COTTAGE RESORT

Circa 1900s After five years as caretaker at Holiday Home Eric Anderson and his wife purchased land in Williams Bay in 1893 and there operated the Fernwood Resort for 37 years. From an old Fernwood brochure "Fernwood is an old Indian camp ground situated on a hill overlooking beautiful Geneva Lake. All rooms are light and airy. Sanitary toilets and bathroom in main building. Electric lights on grounds and in all cottages. Room rates: $24 - $40 per week. Daily rate: $4.50 - $7. Dinners: $1 - $1.25. Boats furnished free to guests.

Photo credits: John A. Anderson.

215

CLARENDELL HOTEL

Circa 1930s Mrs. and Mrs. Carl Ridell purchased Fernwood Inn from Eric Anderson and renamed it the Clarendell Hotel. It sat on the rise of ground on the west side of Walworth Avenue near Elm Street. The Clarendell boasted having large airy rooms, running water, lake beach, and pier. Excellent food and homelike atmosphere. Over the years the exterior of the Clarendell Hotel was modified and in the late 1960s or the early 1970s the owners of the home removed the upper floors.

A guest favorite was Mrs. Ridell's Hungarian Goulash. The recipe was printed in the May 18, 1933 issue of the Bay Leaves.

Mrs. Ridell's Hungarian Goulash

2 lbs round steak	2 TBSP paprika
1/4 lb pork cut in squares	1/2 tsp salt
1 lb onions	

Brown onion first then add the meat and brown both; then add other ingredients and let simmer for 2 hours. Water may be added sparingly as needed. Serve with rice, noodles, or dumplings.

Winter 1933 View from the Clarendell Hotel. Photo credit: Deborah Dumelle Kristmann Collection.

216

FERNDALE INN

Circa 1920 The Ferndale Inn was built by Reverend George Chainey in 1902 as Mahanain Home and School of Interpretation. When Reverend Chainey left Williams Bay for California his home was sold to P. G. Nuernberger and later to Harvey Hatch. Hatch's daughter Edith was manager in the 1930s. Photo credit: Deborah Dumelle Kristmann Collection.

WHEN you plan that much anticipated vacation, or when you're thinking of a nice spot to spend a pleasurable week-end, you'll act wisely by considering FERNDALE INN. Located directly on Williams Bay—overlooking one of the most beautiful parts of Lake Geneva, the INN offers you the happy combination of urban conveniences and every joy of the Great Outdoors.

The surroundings are ideal for a quiet, restful and healthful vacation or holiday. Beautiful walks and drives through thick-wooded hills and fine highways give guests the opportunity to see many nearby points of interest.

FERNDALE INN has large, comfortable rooms, spacious porches, hot and cold spring water in all bath rooms. The cuisine is excellent, recommended by Duncan Hines in "Adventures in Good Eating."

Only two hours from the Chicago Loop. Four blocks from Chicago and Northwestern Railway, Williams Bay Postoffice and garage. All public lake boats stop at the Pier on their trips around this most wonderful and scenic lake.

FERNDALE INN

Williams Bay, Wisconsin

SOMERSET LODGE

After the Ferndale Inn burned Somerset Lodge was built in its place; notice the same stone arch facade. Photo credit: Michelle Bie Love.

217

MAPLE GROVE RESORT

Circa 1930s Maple Grove Resort and Tea Room was located on Elmhurst Street and featured German home cooking featuring a chicken dinner served family style for 85¢. Maple Grove Resort was owned by A. Kaukol and was later known as Krueger's Maple Grove Resort and Tea Room Photo credit: Michelle Bie Love.

REST COTTAGE RESORT

Circa 1930s Located on the corner of Cherry and Clover Streets Rest Cottage Resort was owned and operated by Mrs. Charles J. Jensen. Mrs. Jensen provided guests with comfortable rooms and delicious meals. Photo credit: Michelle Bie Love.

NORMANDIE HOTEL

Circa 1930s J. Noble was the proprietor of the Normandie Hotel located on Walworth Avenue. The Normandie Hotel offered guests reasonable rates and home-cooked meals as well as a year-round coffee shop managed by Mrs. Elizabeth Singer. Photo credit: Deborah Dumelle Kristmann Collection.

SHERWOOD RESORT

Circa 1930s Sherwood Resort was located on the northwest corner of Cherry and Clover Streets. S. and L. Lundberg were the proprietors. The resort offered guests American and European plan rates. Rooms were $1.75 to $3 per day or $12.50 to $14.50 by the week. Guests were served dinner at a cost of 50¢ on weekdays and a full course "Spring Chicken" dinner on Sunday for 75¢. Photo credit: Deborah Dumelle Kristmann Collection.

ROSE LANE LODGE

Circa 1920s Proprietor J. Jorgensen offered guests at Rose Lane Lodge on the shore of beautiful Geneva Lake comfortable, modern, airy rooms, hot and cold running water, a fine beach, free boats to guests staying for a week, and two 4-room housekeeping cottages. Rates: $15 - $25 per week per person. Dinners were served daily and on Sunday.

Photo credit: Deborah Dumelle Kristmann Collection.

LAKE LANE FARM

Lake Lane Farm was so named because one could follow the lane from the farm to Hill Street, down Cherry Street and to the lake.

Gus and Hilma Johnson opened their farm to guests in 1912. The farm house was small, two rooms down and two rooms up, one bath and three large screen porches. The old kitchen of the house was removed and used as a guest house with a small screen porch added to it. Tents were pitched: one for the guys and one for the gals on the grassy lawn with large trees for shade. Later a bunk house-type cottage was built to accommodate more guests. An outhouse was used to supplement the one bathroom. As many as 40 guests could stay at the farm at one time.

Besides offering guests a bed, the Johnson's served delicious home-cooked meals to their guests. On Sundays guests with a reservation (up to 100 people) would enjoy Hilma's fried chicken dinner with homemade biscuits. Tables were set up on the porches, in the living, dining room, and any other available spot. Sunday dinner cost $1.

Circa 1930s The "kids" at the Lake Lane Farm mailbox. Front Left to Right: Arthur Dyrness, Elsie Johnson, Dena Dyrness Johnson. Back Left to Right: Burt Dyrness, Helmer Johnson, Alvin Johnson
Photo credits: Curt Carlson.

Circa 1892 Gus and Hilma Johnson, immigrants from Sweden, met in the United States and were married in 1892. They purchased William Tully's 70 acre farm on Theatre Road in 1907.

HOTEL WILLIAMS BAY

Gus Hawkinson and Eric Werner opened the Hotel Williams Bay in the old frame school on the corner of Colllie and Congress Streets. The advertisement below is from the August 23, 1921 Chicago Daily Tribune.

"On Friday, September 29, 1922 a fire destroyed the Hotel Williams Bay (formerly the Williams Bay School)." As reported in the Janesville Gazette on October 2, 1922 "A $10,000 loss was sustained by owners when the Williams Bay Hotel burned to the ground Friday night. The loss is partially covered by $5,000 insurance. The fire started in the attic. Owners are Eric Werner and Gus Hawkinson."

This fire occurred prior to the formation of the Volunteer Fire Department in 1923 but even then men from around the Village quickly volunteered to help put out the fire.

1922 Photograph by George Blakslee. Photo credit: Williams Bay School Alumni Association.

Chapter 9

FRESH AIR RETREATS
CAMPS/RELIGIOUS CONFERENCES

In response to the rise of industrialization and the dismal summer conditions in urban communities during the late 1800s, social reform groups brought children from poor neighborhoods in large cities like Chicago to the Geneva Lake for "Fresh Air" camps. Most of these Fresh Air camps combined outdoor sports and recreation with religious foundations in which to nurture the faith of the youth.

Early American religious camps (primarily Christian) were heavily influenced by two definitive religious movements: the camp meeting and the religious conference. During the period of western expansion in this country, many of the religious needs of people were met through camp meetings. These outdoor gatherings provided both social and religious opportunities for people living far from one another.

Religious conferences formed the next major development of religious camps. The Chautauqua Conferences were founded by Methodists at Chautauqua Lake in New York as a training institute for Sunday school teachers. It is credited with being the influential foundation for other conferences that came later. These conferences included lectures on Sunday school work, teacher meetings, prayer services, children programs, and sermons. Focus was on the commitment of educating the total person.

Williams Bay has been home to some of the oldest religious and recreational camp organizations on Geneva Lake - some dating back to the mid- to late-1800s. While each organization served different purposes, their common belief was that fellowship in nature has beneficial effects that linger far beyond the "camp" experience.

CAMP COLLIE

Circa 1895 Camp Collie was the earliest example of a "church camp" on Geneva Lake. It began as an informal camping retreat for members of a Delavan church named for its founder, Reverend Joseph Collie.

Dr. Collie was born on the bank of the Dee in Aberdeenshire, Scotland on Nov. 4, 1824, his father dying the same night. His mother was left with the infant and two older sons to care for. In 1836 they came to America and settled in Kane County, Illinois. Determined to obtain an education, Collie entered Mineral Point Academy and in the fall of 1846 entered was then known as Beloit Seminary, graduating Valedictorian of his class of five four years later. Collie then entered Andover Theological Seminary, graduating in1854. He served at the Congregational Church in Delavan for 41 years. In 1873, Collie purchased several acres on the western tip of Williams Bay (now known as Conference Point) where he and his colleagues and their families camped. This marked the beginning of Camp Collie.

Photo credits: Deborah Dumelle Kristmann Collection, United Church of Christ Delavan, and Lake Geneva Picturesque and Descriptive.

SUNDAY SCHOOL/CONFERENCE POINT CAMP

After Reverend Collie's death in 1904, his son W.R. "Win" Collie sold the camp to E. H. Nicols who renamed it the Lake Geneva Sunday School Association and then later Conference Point. "Win" continued to run the camp until 1914.

At left is Invitation Way, the drive to Congress Club and Conference Point circa early 1900s.

Photo credits: Deborah Dumelle Kristmann Collection; Williams Bay Historical Society.

CONFERENCE POINT CAMP

In 1913, the International Training School for Sunday School leaders acquired Conference Point with the intent to use the facility for training its youth leaders. In 1918, the neighboring Dronley estate was purchased from W. J. Chalmers, expanding the camp to 30 acres with one-half mile of shore frontage.

In 1922, the International Council of Religious Education took over Conference Point and it was run by the National Council of Churches.

Campers returned to Conference Point Camp year after year. From the youngest camper to the oldest they were a family.

The photo top right shows the 1934 camp family. Campers would gather at

the dining hall, chapel, Horsley fountain, and the administration building to visit with friends they had not seen since the summer before. No trip to Conference Point Camp would have been complete without standing on Plymouth Rock at the Point.

Photo credits: Deborah Dumelle Kristmann Collection; Beautiful Lake Geneva; Sheilia Cisco; Nancy Snidtker Baldwin, Williams Bay Historical Society.

HOLIDAY HOME FRESH AIR ASSOCIATION

Circa 1888 Holiday Home was established in 1887 by Chicago industrialists and seasonal residents. It remains one of the oldest accredited camps in the country still operating in its original location. Holiday Home was founded on the premise of allowing a camp experience in fresh air and nature to the less fortunate children of Chicago.

The association purchased a 12-acre strip of land, 275 feet wide on the shoreline northeast of Forest Glen Park for $4,000. A three-story building was built to accommodate 75 children. The first building was finished in July 1888. Also built were a caretaker's house and a cottage for the summer staff. Dedication services were held on July 5, 1887, with Professor David Swing officiating.

Photo credits: John A. Anderson.

One of the early supporters was Edward E. Ayer. Both Mr. and Mrs. Ayer were deeply committed to The Lake Geneva Fresh Air Association. Another early supporter was Richard Teller Crane, founder of Crane Company. Over the years the Crane family continued to support Holiday Home Camp through the contributions of Dorothy Crane Maxwell and Augustus K. Maxwell. A cabin was named Maxwell in their honor. Through the years there have been many social occasions to benefit the camp. One of the finest was the dance to celebrate the opening of Holiday Home. In 1904, the first Mid-summer Fair was held at the Levi Leiter estate to benefit Holiday Home.

In the early years, young working women attended special camp sessions and mothers often attended camp with their children.

Photo credits: Holiday Home; Deborah Dumelle Kristmann Collection; and Michelle Bie Love.

229

YMCA CAMP

William Lewis   Robert Weidensall   I.E. Brown

As early as 1872, Robert Weidensall, the International Secretary of the YMCA, had been interested in the idea of establishing a training center for Young Men's Christian Association workers. In June

1884, during the YMCA Secretaries' Conference at Camp Collie in Williams Bay, Weidensall met Isaac E. Brown and William E. Lewis. The Western Secretaries Institute of the YMCA was the vision of I. E. Brown, William Lewis, and Robert Weidensall, YMCA leaders commissioned to develop the movement in the western United States.

The campus thrived as YMCA workers from across the country gathered for physical activity, spiritual reflection and service learning. The training camp grew rapidly, and it moved to the Hyde Park neighborhood of Chicago in 1890 and became an institution of higher learning for students entering human service professions such as parks and recreation, education, and social work.

The Lake Geneva campus served as a "college camp" used for retreats. With growth and popularity, the institution expanded; more land was acquired and buildings were added.

In 1896 the Institute merged with the Chicago campus and renamed The Secretarial Institute and Training School of the YMCA. The first permanent camp building was Lewis Auditorium (above) in 1890. Other early buildings were Weidensall Administration building and the Women's Building (below) built in 1929 and renamed for Mabel Cratty, the first general secretary of the YWCA in the 1930s.

In 1913, the name of the institution changed to The Young Men's Christian Association College. In 1933 the camp was renamed George Williams

College Camp in honor of the founder of the YMCA organization in England during the early nineteenth century.

Kish-Wau-Ke-Tok Golf Club was added in 1901. Edwin B. Frost was a charter member and the first winner of the Club's Spaulding Cup in 1902. The golf club quickly became a six-hole course and by 1929, with the growing popularity of the sport, the course was expanded to 18 holes.

Photo credits: Deborah Dumelle Kristmann Collection, Williams Bay Historical Society, and Aurora University.

ELEANOR CAMP

The founder of the Eleanor Foundation, Ina Law Robertson, was a contemporary of legendary reformer Jane Addams. As the Chicago Tribune reported in 2001, Eleanor residences "provided inexpensive, dormitory-style housing for single women," and at the nonprofit's zenith in the early 1900s "Eleanor was a vast social organization, there were Eleanor banking facilities, an Eleanor League for girls, an Eleanor monthy magazine, and an Eleanor Camp in Lake Geneva."

In 1908, Robertson addressed a different need: women were shut out of all of the downtown-based clubs in Chicago, Robertson launched a social, educational, and philanthropic club called Central Eleanor Club where working women could gather. At its peak there were over 2,000 members involved in classes, language lessons, and drama clubs.

In 1909, Robertson next launched the Eleanor Camp, a vacation getaway

Dining Hall, The Eleanor Camp, Lake Geneva, Wis.

Interior—Recreation Hall, Eleanor Camp, Lake Geneva, Wis.

for women on Geneva Lake. This first site was just east of Black Point. In 1913 the Eleanor Foundation purchased land in Williams Bay, establishing a permanent vacation camp for young women who were self-supporting and of good moral character whether a member of the Eleanor Club or not. The vacationing women enjoyed steamer excursions, fishing, tennis, archery, croquet, picnics in the woods, and other diversions of camp life. Camp literature suggested "a good camping outfit is composed of middy waists and knickers or short skirt, bathrobe, warm wrap, heavy low heeled shoes, rubbers, rain coat, bathing suit, flashlight, and guitar, mandolin or ukulele for girls who play."

Photo credits: Deborah Dumelle Kristmann Collection.

OLIVET CAMP

In 1908 Dr. Norman B. Barr was a speaker at a conference held at the YMCA Camp. During his visit, he walked along the shore path past a piece of property advertised for sale by Alice B. Stockman, M.D. He immediately viewed the property as ideal for a permanent camp for Olivet Institute. The property was identified as lots 1, 2, 3, and 28 in Grand Terrace Subdivision. The property included six acres of land, buildings, and 375 feet of frontage on Geneva Lake. Reverend Barr borrowed $50 for a down payment from a colleague, Olaf O. Anderson, a

deacon and elder at Olivet Church. Olivet Summer Assembly Association was the new owner and the site became known as Olivet Camp.

Members of the Olivet Institute community would take the train to Williams Bay where they transferred to boats that took them to Olivet Camp. Housing at the time consisted of tents and water was transported from a spring at neighboring Holiday Home. Kerosene was used for lighting and cooking. Food requiring refrigeration was stored in the ground until an ice house was built. As cottages replaced tents, a sewer system and electricity were added, showers were built, and the grounds were developed.

Photo credits: Norman B. Barr Camp.

ROCKFORD CAMP

Rockford Camp provided a summer retreat for the Josiah Leonard and Milton Brown families that continued for six generations. Located between Eleanor Camp and the YMCA Camp on "useless lakefront" land owned by farmer Joseph Stam. This land was known as Stam's Woods and later Dartmouth Woods.

Leonard and Brown leased land from Joseph Stam in 1888 for the camp. The original camp consisted of tents with wood floors, and a barn that served as the camp kitchen and dining room. An ice house and outhouses were located behind the tents. Water was carried from Collie Spring.

Families attended church services and activities at Camp Collie and the YMCA Camp. This was the start of Rockford Camp. Eventually 10 small cottages were built and by 1921 each cottage had a kitchen and bathroom facilities. The families of Rockford Camp enjoyed the relaxed lifestyle at the lake with activiites that included music, plays, card games, picnics, water sports, and shore path walks.

The Rockford Camp property was sold in 1975.

Photo credits: *Camps of Geneva Lake*, Carolyn Smeltzer and Jill Westberg, Arcadia Publishing, 2016.

238

Chapter 10

GENEVA LAKE HISTORICAL SOCIETY
CENTENNIAL CELEBRATION
1831-1931

"Sometime in the fall of 1926 or the spring of 1927 Dr. Paul B. Jenkins of Williams Bay and S.B. Chapin of Lake Geneva found themselves on a train from Lake Geneva to Chicago discussing early Geneva Lake history. Dr. Jenkins published the *Book of Lake Geneva* in 1922 and S. B. Chapin was deeply involved in the establishment of the Lake Geneva Water Safety Patrol. Both had active interests in the lake and its history determined that it would be prudent to mark some of the earliest significant landmarks of the Geneva Lake region" (Milwaukee Journal, October 25, 1931). Out of the exchange between Jenkins and Chapin the Geneva Lake Historical Society was formally established on September 23, 1927.

Other prominent residents, including J. S. Hotton, Edward C. Jenkins, Edwin B. Frost, M. A. Healy, Dr. M. A. Healy, Dr. Otto L. Schmidt, Storrs B. Barrett, and H. B. Bensen. Members were eager to help organize the society and expand the reach of the society's efforts to collect and preserve materials of historic significance to the Geneva Lake area. They began by erecting markers at early Geneva Lake historic sites.

On July 28, 1927 in conjunction with the Lake Geneva Air and Water Regatta, the founders of the Geneva Lake Historical Society accomplished their first goal with the formal dedication of five bronze tablets, attached to boulders taken from the quarry in Fontana, marking the sites connected with the Potawatomi village and the first documented visit of whites to the lake in 1831.

- **Marker No. 1** is located where the old Indian trail from the foot of Lake Michigan approached Geneva Lake. The marker bears this inscription: "The old Indian trail from the foot of Lake Michigan to Lake Geneva and on to "the four lakes" at Madison–part of a primitive system that practically crossed the continent–passed here."

- **Marker No. 2** Glenwood Springs, the site where Kinzie Parly first saw the lake on their initial trip here in May 1831 and bears the following inscription: "The old Indian trail from the foot of Lake Michigan to Lake Geneva passed a short distance north of this point. From it the first whites saw the lake May 1831."

- **Marker No. 3** Buena Vista Club in Fontana, the inscription reads: "A village of Potawatomi Indians occupied the rising ground just west of this spot. Their intention to join the hostiles in the Blackhawk war of 1832 was defeated by Shabbona, an Ottawa Indian, friendly to the whites, who here discovered the post and warned the settlers. The Indian Lands about the lake were purchased by the United States at the great Indian council in Chicago 1833 and the Indians were removed to western reservations in 1836."

- **Marker No. 4** Big Foot and Kinzie Streets in Fontana, the inscription reads: "The lodge of Big Foot, chief of the local Potawatomi village, stood a few feet south of this point"

- **Marker No. 5** Big Foot Country Club in Fontana, the inscription reads: "Chief Big Foot and the Potawatomi Indians deemed these seven pools the abode of spiritual beings with power for good and evil in human affairs. No expedition of hunting or war was begun without here asking their favor." Marker photo credits: Big Foot Country Club.

In 1929, the Geneva Lake Historical Society grew to more than 100 individuals and was one of the most active historical societies in the State of Wisconsin. That year they dedicated a historical marker commemorating the sacred burial site of the wives of Chief Big Foot in Williams Bay. At that event they announced their future goals: the desire to establish a museum to house the many artifacts that fell into the society's possession, a dedicated camp site for visiting native

Potawatomi, the commission of a comprehensive archeological survey of the Geneva Lake region including Como by Dr. Charles E. Brown, director of the State Historical Museum at Madison, followed by a publication detailing their findings, and a Centennial celebration for the year 1931, marking the hundredth anniversary of the Kinzie party's arrival to the shores of Geneva Lake.

Plans for the Geneva Lake Centennial began in the fall of 1930 with a committee of forty members that included involvement of local schools, clubs, and organizations. Plans for a two-day event to take place on Friday, June 26th and Saturday June 27th, 1931 commenced. The objective of the Centennial celebration was an educational review of the progress of the previous century.

The Geneva Lake Centennial Executive Committee: W.S. Perrigo, Chairman, L.E. Myers, Treasurer, A.G. Bullock, Assistant Treasurer, J.S. Hotton, Manager. Committee members: Otto L. Schmidt, Paul B. Jenkins, B.B. Bell, S.B. Chapin, Wm. Wrigley, Jr., Col. Wm. Nelson Pelouze, Robert Tarrant, S.P. Taggart, Geo. Van Biesbrock, John Brennan, Ralph Bucknall, Leonard Church, Mrs. Marie Host, Edward Dunn, and Miss Maud Mitchell, Superintendent of Walworth County Schools.

The One Hundredth Anniversary of the Kinzie party arrival was celebrated at the three municipalities around the lake—Lake Geneva, Williams Bay, and Fontana in June of 1931. With a crowd estimated at over 20,000, the Centennial began with an illuminated marine parade of watercraft on the lake, followed by fireworks on Friday night. The next morning, the opening of a Centennial Historical Exhibit took place at the Williams Bay Public Library. The historical exhibit included an abundance of relics from the Potawatomi and the early pioneers. These relics told a story of early methods of work and fashions in dress. The Potawatomi relics and pioneer implements display was so extensive that the Geneva Lake Historical Society insured its value at $10,000.

Dr. Louise Kellogg of the State Historical Society made an opening address and Miss Fay Brink, daughter of John Brink, the government surveyor who first surveyed the lake and renamed it Geneva ninety-four years prior was presented. Professor of Anthropology Alonzo K. Pond, previously from the Department of Anthropology of Beloit

College, presented an exhibition of the methods for the manufacture of flint arrow and spear heads used by Native Americans.

In Fontana, the Centennial Celebration was punctuated by a dramatic reenactment of the Kinzie party's arrival to what was then called Big Foot Lake. Actors impersonated the Kinzie party, all in appropriate clothing of the time, equipped, mounted, and armed. The reenactment also showed the interesting and dramatic incident of the "unknown French trader" who is known to have visited the lake prior to 1836; John Brink, the government surveyor, whose reenactor carried the original instrument with which the survey work was done; the illiterate first frontiersman and Indian-fighter, Christopher Payne; Reverend A. S. Dwindle, the first missionary of the region; and the first covered wagon of incoming settlers. Thirty-two Potawatomi men, women, and children from Forest County in northern Wisconsin, direct descendants of the Potawatomi from Chief Big Foot's villages, impersonated their ancestors. They were dressed in their best tribal regalia—one wore little else than his leggings, beads, head-dress, and his beloved insignia, a white swan's wing.

It is estimated that 3,000 automobiles were parked in the streets of Fontana, a small village of about 300 inhabitants at that time. Some 12,000 people were said to have witnessed the pageant and all was captured on film by the direction of Mr. Harley Clark, President of the Fox Film Company and local summer resident. Full "sound movies" of the entire pageant were taken; to be preserved in the archives of the Society for the interested study of generations to come (Wisconsin Archeologist, Vol. 11, No. 2; The Geneva Lake Centennial, Paul B. Jenkins).

[Note: The Geneva Lake Historical Society disbanded by the mid 1930s, the whereabouts of the Fox film documenting the Centennial Celebration of 1931, the collection of historically significant artifacts and relics of the Potawatomi and early settlers remains unknown today.]

1927 DEDICATION HISTORIC MARKERS

July 28, 1927 Ceremonial dedication of the five bronze tablets, attached to boulders marking the sites connected with the Potawatomi village and the first documented visit of whites to the lake in 1831. Chief Whitefeather speaking to the assembled audience. Photo credit: Big Foot Country Club.

July 28, 1927 Dedication of the historical markers in Fontana. Photo credit: Big Foot Country Club.

July 28, 1927 Paul Burrill Jenkins speaking at the dedication of the five markers commemorating the locations of Chief Big Foot's village and other significant early locations, Jenkins was the author of several books including *The Book of Lake Geneva*. Paul B. Jenkins died at his home in Williams Bay on August 4, 1936.

Jenkins was a descendant of John Jenkins of Plymouth, Massachusetts (1635) and Revolutionary War captain, Ebenezer Jenkins. Paul Jenkins was a Chaplin during WW I and a minister at Immanuel Presbyterian Church in Milwaukee. Photo credit: Barrett Memorial Library.

July 28, 1927 At the Fontana lakeshore for the unveiling of the Potawatomi village marker at the location of Buena Vista Club. Photo credit: Big Foot Country Club.

DEDICATION OF THE SACRED POTAWATOMI BURIAL GROUND ON ELM STREET JUNE 6, 1929

June 6, 1929 Before the Centennial Celebration in 1931, Chief Simon Kahquados, last hereditary Chief of the Wisconsin Potawatomi people, visited the sacred burial ground on Elm Street. Two of Chief Big Foot's wives and several of his children were buried here after the terrible whooping cough [Pertussis] epidemic that affected the area and claimed the lives of many members of Chief Big Foot's tribe. Chief Simon Kahquados, last hereditary Chief of the Wisconsin Potawatomi People and a band of 20 of his tribe spent a week honoring the Potawatomi holy places around the lake (Cedar Point, Sacred Burial Ground, and the Seven Sacred Springs) performing tribal rites for their ancestors. Photo credits: Forest County Potawatomi Cultural Center, Library & Museum and Barrett Memorial Library.

1929 Chief Kahquados and Dr. Edwin B. Frost, head of the Lake Geneva Historical Society, which sponsored placing the stone marker commemorating the sacred burial ground. Chief Kahquados died on November 27, 1930 near Blackwell, Wisconsin at the age of 79. A year earlier Chief Kahquados had expressed a wish to be buried in Williams Bay with his ancestors in the sacred burial ground; however his burial took place in Door County just outside Peninsula State Park. Photo credit: Barrett Memorial Library.

1931 CENTENNIAL CELEBRATION

1931 Remote phones (and fans) wired in to assist the event coordinators during the Centennial Celebration in Fontana. Mrs. Blake Bell and Mrs. Megran were active philanthropists who were among the many that were involved in the effort to organize the festivities. Photo credit: Big Foot Country Club.

1931 Thirty-two Potawatomi men, women, and children from Forest County in northern Wisconsin, direct descendants of the Potawatomi from Chief Big Foot's villages. They were dressed in their best tribal regalia for the celebration. Photo credit: Big Foot Country Club.

1931 The display of historical items at the Williams Bay Library opened on Saturday morning June 27, 1931. The items in the display were so valuable the Centennial Committee insured them for $10,000 and had a guard on duty 24 hours a day. Photo credit: Big Foot Country Club.

1931 Potawatomi men, women, and children came from Forest County to help celebrated the Geneva Lake Centennial. Photo credit: Big Foot Country Club.

1931 Potawatomi from Forrest County, Wisconsin were in attendance to help set the scene of the Centennial Celebration, recreating a time when their relatives lived upon the lake. They wore their traditional clothing, set up tepees and wigwams made of bark and skins, and cooked their meals over camp fires. They also demonstrated the art of making their baskets, moccasins, and bows and arrows. Photo credit: Big Foot Country Club.

1931 The historical pageant re-enacting the coming of the Kinzie party, on the exact site of their arrival on the west shore. Excitement filled the air as the Potawatomi sang their songs, beat their tom-toms, whirled through their ecstatic dances, sprinkled their incense upon the moving waters, and offered up worship to the spirits. Photo credit Big Foot Country Club.

1931 The crowd attending the celebration were fascinated watching the ceremonies and customs of the Potawatomi people. Photo credit: Big Foot Country Club.

1931 The recreation of the coming of the Kinzie Party to Big Foot (Geneva Lake) was the concluding event of the Centennial Celebration in Fontana. It was estimated that 5,000 were in attendance for that event, which was clearly more than anyone expected. Photo credit: Big Foot Country Club.

249

1931 Scene from the Centennial pageant. Chief Big foot bidding farewell to Mrs. Catherine Van Slyke, wife of the first settler in the vicinity of the Potawatomi village just before leaving the lake in September 1836. Chief Big Foot is impersonated by Chief Shawno of Forest County, Wisconsin. Mrs. Van Slyke is impersonated by Miss Hallie Van Slyke, great-granddaughter of Mrs. Van Slyke. Photo credit: Big Foot Country Club.

1931 At the Seven Sacred Springs on the grounds of Big Foot Country Club, the Potawatomi re-enacted the primitive rites of their forefathers. The Seven Sacred Springs are an unusual conjunction of seven spring-fed pools, close together and naturally arranged in descending steps on a beautiful slope near the lake. A long-established custom of the Potawatomi was to come to the Seven Sacred Springs to pray on every important event of either chase or warfare. This touching observance has been enacted twice—once by the Chief Kahquados in June 1929 and by the Potawatomi who came to participate in the Centennial. The location was marked with a huge boulder with a bronze tablet describing the ancient significance of the spot and commemorating the Centennial and the performance of their ancient worship. Photo credit: Big Foot Country Club.

This McCormick Reaper "model 1836", invented by Cyrus Hall McCormick, was prominently displayed at the Centennial Celebration exhibit. An old man attending the celebration still remembered that he had seen the old-fashioned cradle put to use in the fields in his youth, saying, "And by gosh! A man had to be pretty good in order not to knock his shins as he swung it back and forth."

Source of quote and photo credit: Lake Geneva Regional News, July 1931.

IN MEMORY OF THE PIONEERS
OF OLD WALWORTH

Anchored off in the Pioneer's moorings,
In the land where maps are unknown,
In the land of the beautiful mornings,
In the land where they never go home.
Your memory comes back through the vista,
Across the sand bars and shallows of time,
And we forget about years and distinction,
For there's naught but the soul of Lang Syne.

For the hand of our God is still weaving,
The texture and garments of truth,
We are brothers in all of life's dreamings,
We're the heirs of Eternal youth.

You cannot return from your home land,
For the shoals roar as reckless as Fate,
But the band of the Master still tells us,
There's a welcome, when we open the gate.

Till then Pioneers of old Walworth;
Hail and Farewell!

John E. Burton, early pioneer of Geneva Lake and Walworth County. Written for the Pioneer Day Celebration in 1925.

BIBLIOGRAPHY

BOOKS

Annals of Lake Geneva 1835-1897 (1897), James Simmons

Camps of Geneva Lake (2016), Carolyn Smeltzer and Jill Westberg

Discover Lake Geneva: A Guide to the Historic Lakefront Homes (2003), Lake Geneva Cruise Line

Full Speed Ahead -The Story of the Steamboat Era on Lake Geneva (1972), Larry Larkin

Geneva Lake (2014), Carolyn Hope Smeltzer and Martha Kiefer Cucco

Geneva Lake Are Intensive Survey: An Architectural/Historic Report (1985), Patricia Butler and Sharon Crawford,

Grassroots—Lake Geneva: An illustrated history of the Geneva Lake area (1986), Phil Fogle

History and Indian Remains of Lake Geneva and Lake Como (1930), Paul B. Jenkins and Charles E. Brown

History of Geneva, Wisconsin (1875), James Simmons

History of Walworth County, Wisconsin (1912), Albert Clayton Beckwith

Lake Geneva - Newport of the West 1870-1920 (1976), Ann Wolfmeyer and Mary Burns Gage

Lake Geneva in Vintage Postcards (2005), Carolyn Hope Smeltzer and Martha Kiefer Cucco

Meandering Around Walworth County Volume V - Villages of Fontana and Williams Bay (1995), Ginny Hall

Partick Joseph Healy Founder of the House of Lyon & Healy: An Appreciation, (1907)

Shawneeawkee Friendly Fontana A Pictorial History of the West End of Geneva Lake (1959, 2005) Arthur B. Jensen

Souvenir from Picturesque Lake Geneva, Wisconsin, Wisconsin Transportation Company (1926), Bonnie Burton Denison

Steam Trains to Lake Geneva: C & NW's Elgin-Williams Bay (2002), P. L. Behrens

The Book of Lake Geneva (1922), Paul B. Jenkins

The Thornley family in Williams Bay, 1920s: On Working the Boats with the Chicago & North Western Railroad to Provide Transport to All (2004), Warren Thornley

The Yerkes Observatory of the University of Chicago (1897), George E. Hale

Wau-Bun The Early Day in the Northwest (1857), Juliette Kinzie

Western Historical Company's History of Walworth County, Wisconsin (1882),

Yerkes Observatory (1914), Edwin B. Frost

Yerkes Observatory 1892-1950 The Birth, Near Death, And Resurrection Of A Scientific Research Institution (1997), Donald E. Osterbrock

H. Sargent Michaels' Guide for Motorists (1905)

Tracks Through Time—A Community Remembers, Geneva Lake Train Project, Badger High School, Lake Geneva, Wisconsin (1989)

75 Years on Geneva Lake: A History of Cedar Point Park 1925-2000

Lake Geneva Yacht Club—2004 Yearbook

Celebrating 100 Years of Church Family 1896-1996, United Church of Christ (Congregational) of Williams Bay

Beautiful Lake Geneva, N. W. Smails Publisher

Dear Neighbor–A Cedar Point Memoir (1925-200), Calvin Kuder

Congress Club: An Enduring Summer Tradition, (2014) Carol Carlson Swed

Lake Geneva, Wisconsin–Short History

The Thornley family in Williams Bay, 1920's: on working boats with the chicago and N.W. railroad to provide transport to all, (2004) Warren Thornley

PUBLICATIONS

Bay Leaves (1933-1941 and 1946-1954), Frank Van Epps, publisher

Delavan Republican (May 10,1906)

First Annual Regatta of the Northwestern Association, Fore 'n' Aft, Vol. 2 (1906)

Lovely Lake Geneva and its Noble Charity, National Magazine (1905).

Northwestern Regatta, Fore 'n' Aft, Vol. 3 (1907)

Williams Bay Library to Mark 40th Year on May 15th, Janesville Daily Gazette (Friday, January 2, 1948).

Williams Bay Observer (1896-1897), William Chauncy Dean, publisher

Brief History of Williams Bay, (1935) Frank Van Epps

Williams Bay–A History, (1896) Williams Bay Observer, William Dean

The History of Williams Bay, Compiled by Mrs. George Van Biesbroeck (1957)

Ice and Refrigeration, A Monthly Review of the Ice, Ice Making, Refrigerating, Cold Storage, and kindred Trades, Vol. XIII No. 5 (1897)

The Lake Geneva Centennial, Paul B. Jenkins,Wisconsin Archaeologist, Volume II No. 2 (1932)

American Magazine (January 1920)

The Astrophysical Journal Vol V No.5 (May 1897)

ONLINE SOURCES

History of the Bicycle, Wikipedia, The Free Encyclopedia. (2017)

Six Degrees of George Chainey; Six Degrees of George Chainey: Kingsford, Maitland and Tindall; George Chainey, Nuclear Fusion, and Homeopathy: Where A Book Can Take Us; The Gnostic: A Chainey-Kimball-Colville Production; This Bulwark of Human Hearts: The By-Laws of the Fraternity of the White Cross, 1885, Marc Demarest, http://ehbritten. blogspot.com. (2017)

Civil War Soliders Database, World War I Soldiers Database, Wisconsin Veterans Museum, State of Wisconsin Department of Veterans Affairs, www.wisvetsmuseum.com. (2017)

ABOUT THE AUTHORS

 Michelle Bie Love was born and raised on the northern edge of Williams Bay in Bay View Hills subdivision. Her family came to the Bay in 1936 when her grandparents, dad and aunt left Chicago; living first as caretakers at Olivet Camp and later on the Charles and Hulda Stam farm just west of the Village.

Michelle and her husband David met and were married in Williams Bay. Though they left the Village in 1982, Michelle has always thought of Williams Bay as home. Their son Mike, daughter-in-law Magen, and granddaughter Melissa live in Michelle's childhood home

In her spare time, Michelle loves to take landscape photographs, delve into the history of Williams Bay and the surrounding area, camping and traveling to new areas. As a taphophile or as a tombstone tourist she prefers to be called, Michelle enjoys exploring and photographing old cemeteries. But most of all she loves to spend time with her granddaughter.

Michelle has a degree in Professional Communications from Gateway Technical College. She also has a degree in Accounting. She works as a freelance writer for various publications and companies around the U.S. and Canada. In addition to her freelance work Michelle designed and is the editor of the Williams Bay Historical Society newsletter and web administrator of the historical society's website.

Michelle and Dave reside in Walworth, Wisconsin with their two dogs Buck and Hunter.

 Deborah Dumelle Kristmann and her husband Kurt have been coming to Wisconsin for most of their lives and to the Geneva Lake area for more than 25 years.

In 2001, they became seasonal residents of Williams Bay when they purchased a little cottage built in 1926, the year when Cedar Point Park had just been subdivided. Deb quickly became enamored with the history of the Geneva Lake area and began collecting images from a national craze known as the "golden age of postcards" (1898-1918). Collecting postcards soon became an obsession, along with antique books, maps, and other memorabilia. With a library of material and the Internet at her fingertips, Deb found that researching the area was like time travel and she became immersed!

When Deb is not lost in the past, she enjoys walking the shore path with her dog Gordy; hanging out in parkway 5 with family, friends and neighbors; kayaking; and looking for antiques.

Deb received a B.S. Degree in Art/Graphic Design from Bradley University in Peoria, Illinois. Deb, Kurt, and their two adult children, Conrad and Joanna, currently reside in Barrington, Illinois. Deb and Kurt hope to become full time residents of Williams Bay in 2018.

Made in the USA
Lexington, KY
05 September 2017